The Delicate Balance
of a Woman's Self-Image

The Delicate Balance
of a
Woman's Self-Image

Barbara Sullivan

Published by

chosen books

FLEMING H. REVELL COMPANY
OLD TAPPAN, NEW JERSEY

Library of Congress Cataloging in Publication Data:

Sullivan, Barbara A.
    The delicate balance of a woman's self-image.

    Includes bibliographies.
    1. Women—Religious life. 2. Women—Psychology. I. Title.
BV4527.S84 1984   248.8'43   84-12717

ISBN 0-8007-9074-X

A Chosen Book
Copyright © 1984, Barbara A. Sullivan
Chosen Books are Published by
Fleming H. Revell Company
Old Tappan, New Jersey
Printed in the United States of America

*This book is dedicated
to the women of the Spirit of God Fellowship
who have walked with me
in the search for balanced wholeness
in God*

Acknowledgments

First of all, I want to thank my friend Marie Dennison, whose helpful insights and additions are interwoven with my thoughts throughout this manuscript. Stu and Bonnie Lorenz also spent many hours reading and typing my manuscript and correcting my numerous misspelled words. I also want to thank Pat Sawyer for her suggestion of the title. Finally, many thanks to Kent Garborg, who was the first person to see potential in my manuscript and David Hazard, my friend and editor at Chosen, who said I could when I felt I couldn't.

Contents

1

Greater Expectations

Many of us women are aware that there is a difference between how we appear on the outside and what we are on the inside. Around others we are careful to act confident and self-assured at the very moment we are struggling with a debilitating sense of failure or uselessness.

My own feelings of inadequacy had bubbled under the surface for years. In so many ways, I set myself up for a terrible emotional explosion—mainly by consistently setting impossible goals for myself. As a child I tried to measure up to my brilliant big brother, never able to achieve his good grades. As a teenager I sought unending popularity, and in college I battled for success as the only woman in a competitive pre-med curriculum. When I married I gave up my dreams for a medical career, confident I could be the perfect wife and mother. But four children in rapid succession toppled those dreams of domestic achievement. Even as a new Christian with a growing ministry in our community, I struggled to be the best, the first, the most. More often I felt stranded with no answers to my problems.

I simply was not the me I wanted to be. No matter how hard I tried, no matter what ways I chose to prove to myself I was valuable, my self-image plummeted. The inner pressure built until I felt like a volcano about to explode.

I don't know what finally triggered the explosion. Perhaps it was one more pile of laundry or one more sink full of dirty dishes—more responsibility than my already overloaded system could bear. Whatever the cause, one morning as I poured myself a cup of coffee to calm down, I realized the tension was about to find some kind of release.

My husband had just left for work and I knew I would feel like a fool for bothering him when I couldn't even pinpoint what was wrong with me. Desperate, I dialed his office anyway and left word for him to come back home right away. I had never called him home from work before and I knew he would be worried.

What will I say to him? I thought, as I paced the kitchen floor, the cup of coffee shaking in my hands. I watched the clock until finally I heard a car door slam and hurried steps pad up the sidewalk.

John was barely in the door when he saw me and the state I was in. "What is it, honey? Is it one of the kids? Are you all right?"

I stared at him blankly, grasping for something to say. Then, with rush of tears I blurted out: "I hate myself!"

Stunned, John sat down at the kitchen table, concern on his face, struggling to understand.

I was almost as surprised as John, and truly dismayed at what I heard myself say. But, like bats surprised by light, new thoughts fluttered wildly in my mind seeking escape through my lips.

Tensely gripping the back of a chair, I continued, nearly choking. "I mean it. I hate myself. I've always hated myself. You and the children would be better off if I were dead!"

I knew that John, as a Christian, was a strong believer in the power of prayer, especially when a situation looked impossible. So I was not too surprised when he interrupted me. "Barbara, let's pray about this together."

But I wanted no part of it. "No." I fairly shouted. "Even God can't help me—"

My voice faltered in mid-sentence. The force of my refusal left me dumbstruck. Had I tapped the root of the problem that had troubled me so long?

I collapsed into a chair beside John, still shaking, but somewhat quieter. In the moments that followed, I considered how wide the gap had split between what I knew I *should* be and what I had *tried* to be—my self-imposed, impossible-to-reach image.

On the one hand I knew the Bible said that "when someone becomes a Christian he becomes a brand new person inside. He is not the same anymore. A new life has begun!" (II Corinthians 5:17, LB). On the other hand I didn't feel "new" at all. I felt like a failure from constantly comparing myself with others or setting impossible goals that were bound to produce feelings of worthlessness. The imbalance was too much to bear. It left me frustrated and feeling that I was too tough a case—even for God.

John and I talked and even prayed together that morning. As I watched him drive off once more for the office, I knew that those thoughts had made an impact on me, marking a turning point that was something like an emotional conversion. At the same time, I wondered why my spiritual conversion had not eliminated that inner despair. Was there something more I needed to do?

Over and over since that morning in the kitchen I have seen I was not alone in that imbalance—or that despair—by any means. Women the world over, Christian and non-Christian, are under tremendous pressure to succeed in every one of the many roles of our lives that gauge our sense of self-worth.

Society, for instance, measures our self-worth by questioning "What are you achieving?" rather than "What are you becoming?" We are taught this lesson from the time we enter school. We honor the straight-A student, the star athlete, the cute cheerleader. We choose as our heroes those students who were born beautiful, intelligent or big enough to play football. There are no awards given to the kindest child, the faithful youth, the student who has overcome emotional or physical handicaps. We value achievers not becomers.

Thus, homemakers face constant pressure to abdicate the home and find "true fulfillment" in the working world. We are caught in the controversy between "liberators" like Betty Friedan, who insist women cannot find fulfillment in domesticity, and "total women" like Marabel Morgan, who turn homemaking into a totally plastic experience.

The clamoring voices of the feminists are actually espousing the age-old theory that men *are* superior to women and, in order to find fulfillment, we need to imitate them by entering their world. But neither do the "total women" face the heart of the matter. The question we must answer is: What is my role as a woman in today's world?

Even the Church has clouded the issue by presenting various stereotypes of the Christian woman rather than understanding the needs God has put in us or how to help us find our greatest fulfillment.

When I tried to follow the goals dictated by others rather than search to see what God had planned for my life, I was just widening the huge gap within myself: the gap between the unhappy me on the inside and my "together" appearance on the outside. Once that disparity was acknowledged, I was able to bring my self-image in line with what God intended all along.

Years of prayer and study, struggling and seeking answers have turned up a wealth of riches about the healthy self-image God wants women to have. And these discoveries have held true throughout personal counseling, while teaching seminars or when I am assisting my husband, who leads an interdenominational fellowship. I have seen women from every background—neglected, abused women in inner-city ghettoes, and upper middle class housewives in the suburbs—overcome poor self-images by these principles.

It's what God intended all along.

2

Image vs Reality

I recall going through a fun-house at an amusement park and stopping in front of a distortion mirror. In the rippled silver I looked four feet wide with long, lanky arms, and the features of my face were all askew. Even my laughing expression was distorted; it looked more like a scream of pain.

That was a warped image.

There are mirrors inside of us, too, that can warp the views we have of ourselves. I have discovered three such mirrors: The Mirror of the Past, the Mirror of Self-Expectation, and the Mirror of the Society in which we live.

For me, the Mirror of the Past was especially painful. Every time I looked into it I saw myself at age five on a late spring afternoon. The air was heavy with the sweet odor of honeysuckle which grew on a trellis on our back porch. My friend Cynthia, also five, and I were busy arguing about whose turn it was to be mother that day as we set up our play table for "tea." I picked a few blossoms from the trellis to decorate the table and declared that I would be the mother since it was my back porch, table and tea set.

"Now, Cynthia, it's dinnertime and you have to eat all your dinner before you can go out to play," I said in a near perfect imitation of my mother. I pulled some red berries off a vine and arranged them carefully on her plate. Cynthia gingerly picked one up and pretended to eat it.

"No, don't pretend. You really have to eat them."

"I can't," Cynthia replied. "They're probably poison berries."

"No they're not. I eat them all the time." That was a lie. Somehow, though, I didn't consider the danger if she were right.

"Are you sure?" Cynthia frowned suspiciously.

"Of course I'm sure. Now eat them or you can't go out to play." I spoke sternly and Cynthia brought the bright red berry to her mouth and nibbled it cautiously.

Before long Cynthia's mother called her home to dinner and our game of house was over for the day.

Later that evening, as I was curled up on the couch, listening to my mother read a story, I began to think about what I had done. *You never ate those berries. You made Cynthia eat poison.* A sickening sensation gripped my stomach. *Now she's going to die, and it's all your fault.* I barely heard the story Mother was reading; all I could hear was my heart beating wildly, and my guilty thoughts accusing me. I couldn't tell anyone. To do so would mean admitting I had lied.

"Do you think it's too late to call Cynthia?" I asked before I was sent up to bed. Mother said of course it was much too late.

That was probably the longest night of my life. I was sure I would be awakened by the sound of an ambulance speeding to Cynthia's house next door. What if they woke me up to ask if I had seen her eating anything that might have been poisonous? What would I do? I could hardly stand it until breakfast was over the next morning and I could call Cynthia's house without arousing suspicion. Imagine my relief when Cynthia herself answered the phone.

My friend had survived. But something within me had not. That night, as I faced the darkness inside me, my sense of self-worth shrivelled and died. The realization that I was a bad girl grew with every lie and every act of childhood disobedience. Each wrong motive and action was one more link on a chain which dragged me lower in my own estimation.

Childhood experiences can be powerful convincers of our unworthiness and can cause, among other things, staggering feelings of guilt. Since children interpret experiences differently from adults, they may load their tender emotions with feelings that can last a lifetime. For instance, if children are scolded for being "bad" and never hear their parents say that they are forgiven, they assume that they are unworthy of praise or forgiveness.

Guilt is not caused solely by transgressions on the child's part. It can result from the feelings and interactions between the adults in the household—something over which the child has no control. A child of divorced parents might reason, "If I were a good girl, Dad wouldn't have left." Or, if a child hears arguments about finances, he might think: "If I hadn't been born my parents wouldn't be having money problems now." Children breathe in the emotions their parents exude with the very air of the house. In their immaturity they cannot separate the criticisms and quarrels between their parents from accusations against themselves. And as erroneous as these thoughts are, they are very real and very painful.

Even those children who have suffered the death of a parent, or have been physically abused take on a tremendous amount of guilt. They feel responsible for having caused such behavior in the adults, and for bringing such unhappiness on themselves.

While childhood instances leave some people with a distorted image of overwhelming guilt and worthlessness, such as I had, others will mask over what they see in the inner Mirror of the Past.

I saw this illustrated clearly in Christine, a woman who seemed dedicated to keeping herself beautiful. She was tall and slender with a body that showed the benefits of daily exercise. Her hair was styled in the latest fashion, and frosted with blond highlights. Her nails were long and red, she wore an expensive designer outfit, and even her voice was intentionally soft and cultured. She and her husband of fifteen years had no children; she had made it clear she didn't care to have children. She seemed totally self-centered.

When she came to me for counseling, I found myself wrestling with the feelings of inferiority that always needled me in her presence. Undoubtedly I was threatened, even jealous, of this perfect-looking woman, but she had come to me for help and I had to lay my own feelings aside. As I did, I learned more about her inner motivations for keeping such a perfect facade and felt chagrined at my unkind thoughts toward her.

Christine was reared by a widowed mother who had all she could handle to keep them in groceries. She always felt the other girls in school looked down on her because of the hand-me-down clothes she wore.

One day her mother bought her a brand new white dress. She could hardly wait until the next morning. She skipped to the bus stop with a new sense of self-worth.

When the other girls arrived, however, one of them devised some sort of game, and Christine was "it." They ran up behind her, tapped her on the back and ran away laughing. Christine had no idea why they were laughing, and felt confused. Were they laughing at her? At her new dress? She had hoped she would fit in. She tried to be a good sport and laugh with them, but an ache was beginning to grow inside her. She was relieved when the school bus arrived and the game was over.

All day at school she felt that others were laughing and pointing at her behind her back, but it wasn't until she returned home that she found out why. The girls at the bus stop had apparently rubbed their hands in the dirt before they tapped her, and the entire back of her beautiful white dress was covered with dirty smudges. All day she had walked through school not knowing that she was the target for jokes and humiliation. Shame flooded through her as she remembered how proud she had felt in her new dress. What a fool she had been. A huge gap opened between the way she wanted to appear and how she felt others saw her. She resolved inwardly to spend the rest of her life making sure that nothing in her appearance would cause anyone to laugh at her again.

As a grown woman, Christine looked into the Mirror of her Past and saw the distorted image of a naive little girl who was made to look like a fool, and that image formed the basis for strong achievement goals in her life. Once she verbalized that scene, she was able to understand her drive to succeed, and to work toward a balanced and healthy self-image.

Though we handled it differently, Christine and I were hurt by the Mirror of the Past and turned to view ourselves in a new mirror: the Mirror of Self-Expectation.

This can produce an equally distorted picture. I myself was a quiet, introverted girl with few close friends until I entered high school. There, in that closed social system, I at last spotted an area where I could excel. I became a "joiner" and entered into many of the school's extracurricular activities. In my last year, I was voted the friendliest girl in the senior class. I was out to prove I was not a loser. Certainly the friendliest girl in the class couldn't be all that bad.

In college I joined a prestigious sorority, but soon found that parties, late night dates and being seen at the "right" places left me feeling empty. I grew tired of my shallow life. Being popular was not bringing the expected rewards. I had reached one mountain peak, but found it only an illusion, so I set my sights on a higher peak.

I transferred to a new college in a pre-med curriculum. I would pursue academics. My new school was noted for its academic excellence, and I relished competing against all the boys in the program. My older brother, Tom, had always been applauded by my parents for his high grades, and perhaps it was a way of competing with him.

My new image was that of a serious intellectual. Since I had never been studious, the strain of trying to be a straight-A student proved almost too much. In my fifth year of college, I began having physical symptoms which were diagnosed as manifestations of nervous tension. I was sent home for a two-week rest.

It was during this same last year of school that I became engaged to John, who was a second-year dental school student. Marriage meant giving up my desire of going to medical school, but by this time I was tired of the intellectual image and ready for a new one—that of the world's greatest wife and mother. However, three babies born little more than a year apart and a fourth shortly thereafter crushed my self-expectations. That warped image, too, was doomed.

My life became an endless round of feeding hungry babies and changing dirty diapers. John was so busy establishing his new dental practice that he was never home to help out. Evenings he was either doing his laboratory work or going to meetings to introduce himself to people in the community.

Again a gap opened—this time between my dream image and the realities of motherhood. I became more and more resentful of my lot in life. The only purpose served by my complaints and tears was to drive John away from the house every chance he got. Church work was not yet part of our lives, or he might have buried himself in that as well.

One night after an exceptionally heated argument with John, my sniffles grew more pronounced until tears were running down my face and sobs caught in my throat.

Near hysteria, I retreated into the cocoon of my bed. "It's hopeless," I wept into my pillow. In a few moments, a growing heaviness in my chest was hindering my ability to breathe.

Gasping for air I felt everything begin to close in on me; I had to escape. Throwing off the covers I pulled myself to my feet and stumbled through the hall. The wall clock, the pictures—everything was spinning. In the living room I collapsed on the floor. I had little control over my body and could not seem to stop gurgling noises in my throat.

An alluring, bottomless dark pit seemed to yawn before me, and I lay on crumbling sand at its brink. It was so appealing. All I had to do was drop off in space with one long scream. I could escape, if I chose to, from my crushing responsibilities by letting myself slide into the hell of mental illness. I knew if I made that choice there would be no return.

In that suspended moment of time, I could see that my whole future depended on choosing life—which for me meant continuing to shoulder responsibility—or death. From somewhere came a nudge, a spark of light, the strength to make my choice. Faintly, I managed to whisper, "I want to live."

Immediately I felt as if someone reached down and pulled me back from the crumbling edge of the pit onto solid ground. I lay still for a time, then slowly got to my feet. Weakly I walked back to bed—my first steps back to wholeness.

Although it was five years before I came to know God, whose everlasting arms had reached to me during that crisis, I never again returned to that state of utter desolation.

From then on I tried to be more realistic about the expectations I placed on myself. I found it wasn't so terrible if the children weren't always spotless, or if I weren't the best hostess on the block. Inwardly I was finding a new restfulness, and I might have continued in that vein, but I soon got side-tracked in external trappings and began to look at myself through the third mirror, the Mirror of Society's Values.

Society tells us that it is the external, materialistic goals that, once fulfilled, will make us happy. I began to trade true happiness for the hollowness of outer trappings: our beautiful house in the suburbs, my husband's thriving dental practice, lawns with flower beds, suites of furniture.

If we gaze at a distorted image long enough we eventually come to accept it as truth; we become comfortable with it. Sometimes complacency becomes a good trade-off for reality.

That is how I felt one fall day in 1971 when I stood, dust cloth in hand, in the middle of the family room of our brand new home. Mellow music drifted from the radio, and I looked out through the patio doors to a crisp, beautiful day, with fallen leaves curling on the ground waiting to be raked.

I have it all, I thought. *Everything is as it should be, and yet . . . where is the contentment, the joy I should be feeling on a day like this?*

As if in commiseration, I heard Peggy Lee's voice on the radio sing the popular song, "Is That All There Is?" The words hit home: "Is that all there is to a fire? Is that all there is to a circus?" That was my life Peggy Lee was singing about, and I could expand on it. Is that all there is to a marriage—kissing my husband goodbye in the morning and hello at night without any deeper communication? Is that all there is to a family—this day to day routine of laundry and meals and getting the kids ready for school? Is that all there is to a dream house in the suburbs— vacuuming, dusting and scrubbing floors?

As I polished the desk top I noticed a small appointment calendar. Suddenly, I thought of my life as a calendar, each leaf marking one year. A hand was flipping over leaf after leaf. I knew that, when all the leaves were finally turned, there would be nothing at the end, nothing to give my life meaning. I had spent my time on the externals—worrying about the right house, clothes, cars—hoping to cover up the hollow place within the center of my being. I mistakenly assumed I would like myself if I *had* all the right things, and I almost succeeded in believing I was happy and fulfilled. Seeing through the illusion, I realized that if I were to die at that moment I would have nothing to take into eternity, no part of myself that I felt was worth saving.

That experience made a deep impression on me, but I didn't know what to do about it. If society didn't have the answers, I didn't know where to turn to find them.

Not long after, an unexpected "signpost" pointing in the right direction came from my brother, who had made a new discovery. He had not only embraced the Christian faith, he had had a personal encounter with Jesus. He knew Jesus as his Savior, and it changed his life. John and I could see how real the experience had been for Tom. We both prayed, committing our lives to Christ, as he had done. We knew that the very Spirit of God had come into the center of our lives and re-ordered them. Briefly, I felt clean and renewed.

Immediately, John and I found ourselves in a whirlwind of new activity. I had never been so busy or so satisfied. Friends, impressed by the change in our lives, asked if they could join us for prayer and worship. Scores of people passed through our home over the next several years, enjoying the friendship, joy and familial warmth. Many exciting and miraculous answers to prayer heightened my happiness, for, truly, I was happier than I had ever been.

My life had meaning. And most of all, I believed that the old hurts and frustrations would never have to be dealt with, now that I had found a *new* life.

I was wrong.

Gradually, I recognized unwelcome thoughts slipping into my consciousness. *How can this be?* I murmured again and again as feelings of self-hate and inadequacy hung over me once more. I became depressed and irritable. My joy in discovering the light was soured as more dark clouds rolled in, one after the other.

Because I had never dealt with the gap between how I felt on the inside and how I appeared on the outside, destructive thoughts of my worthlessness were never removed, they were only buried. Even though I was learning, at least in my head, what the Bible meant by calling God my Father, that I was His child and that He loved me, I was still clinging to a broken image, an inner vision of a woman who was too worthless for God to love.

The broken image persisted until that morning in the kitchen when I could bear it no longer and "exploded." Disappointment in my failure had kept me from believing that God really loved me. When I finally accepted the fact that His purposes in teaching me about balance were bound by His love, I no longer had to endure self-imposed standards. I could simply let His image reflect through me, and change me from the inside. I simply asked Him to remove my low opinion of myself, and fill me instead with a reflection of Himself.

As the Apostle Paul says, "We all, with unveiled face beholding as in a *mirror* the glory of the Lord, are being transformed *into the same image* from glory to glory, just as from the Lord, the Spirit" (II Corinthians 3:18, italics added). This is God's purpose in our lives: to destroy all our false images and reproduce *His* image within us.

3

The Balanced Life

This last half of the twentieth century is a time of great confusion among women concerning roles in the home, working world, community and even Church. True, we have greater freedom in our society than we have ever had before, but it is a freedom without clearly defined roles and boundaries.

The Mirror of Society's Values is probably the most difficult image to overcome because of the many and varied voices all claiming the way to liberation. But until we give up this and other false mirrors and determine to follow God's guidelines, we cannot assume our rightful roles.

Noted child psychologist Dr. James Dobson believes a good self-image and sense of personal worth affect not only individuals, but the whole fabric of society:

> . . . whenever the keys to self-esteem are seemingly out of reach for a large percentage of the people, as in twentieth-century America, then widespread "mental illness," neuroticism, hatred, alcoholism, drug abuse, violence, and social disorder will certainly occur. Personal worth is not something human beings are free to take or leave. We must have it and when it is unattainable, everybody suffers.[1]

So how can we go about freeing ourselves from prisons of dissatisfaction, self-hate and poor self-image? What are the "keys" to self-esteem?

As I searched for answers to these questions, I saw that we can be released from the prison of poor self-image by self-acceptance—coming to terms with our lives in the fullest sense, and coming to terms with the Giver of life.

Thus, the first key to a good self-image is simply this: Understand God's love for you and His acceptance.

We must come to see ourselves as objects of God's love. The Bible, one of the oldest books on earth, establishes our worth in the truest and most timely sense: "How great is the love the father has lavished on us, that we should be called children of God!" (I John 4:19). Because God has "lavished" His love on us, we can love and accept ourselves as well as others. "We love because he first loved us" (I John 4:19).

With that basis of trust and love, the second key of self-acceptance becomes easier to grasp: Accept your past.

Rather than thinking of the past as a rope that will wrap you tightly for the rest of your life, realize that God is in charge of *everything* and can use your past for purposes you many never have realized. Look at Romans 8:28: "In *all* things God works for the good of those who love him, who have been called according to his purpose" (italics added). "All things" includes unhappy things from the past, as well as the happy ones.

I have found this to be true time and time again. I remember the first time that I discovered God could make use of the difficult times of my past.

I had spent a productive morning around the house. Beds were made, dishes washed, newspapers smashed in the trash compactor and a load of clothes was chugging away in the washing machine. My daily devotional had referred to Romans 8:28, which had me thinking all morning about how God could possibly find any useful purpose in the self-degrading, competitive, perfectionist person I had been. True, I had learned some valuable spiritual lessons. I had recognized God's love for me, and prayed for His image to be reflected in me. I had come to terms with my identity as a woman, a wife and a mother. And I was grateful that God had brought me out of the tangle I had created. Mostly, though, I just wanted to forget all about it, to put it as far from me as possible. I couldn't imagine what good could ever come out of it.

In the middle of this reflection, I heard a knock at the front door. It was Judy, a young woman from my neighborhood, who asked if we could talk. I led the way into the kitchen where we could visit comfortably over coffee. She sat across from me at the table, her expression drawn and discouraged.

She told me that for years she had struggled to be "all things to all people." She felt it her duty to be a romantic and loving wife, a giving mother, and a close companion and friend to all who needed her. Time she had spent in church had only equipped her with do's and don't's of religion, not a sense of a relationship with God.

"The trouble is," she said, "the harder I try, the more depressed I get. I just feel so hopeless and at times I don't even want to go on living. I'm tired of always feeling guilty."

I was intrigued with her story—it so closely paralleled my own. When she finished, I suggested that she might be trying to compensate for a poor self-image. I told her how, until I had recognized God's loving purpose for my own life, I had not been able to find inner peace. She brightened as I described some of the role conflicts in my own life that had been resolved.

It was deeply rewarding to watch the despair in Judy's face slowly give way to hope. She bowed her head and prayed, asking God to make sense of her life. Then I prayed that she would discover purpose—a rich and meaningful identity as a daughter of God.

After Judy left I was putting our coffee cups in the emptied dishwasher when the thought struck me: The struggles that I had experienced had been my point of identification with Judy. It was precisely because of the unhappy times from my past that I could comfort and encourage her. God answered the questions I had raised that morning by showing me firsthand how He can work "all things" out for good.

That was the first time I saw God using my past in a constructive way, but by no means the last. I found that the problems I had experienced were common to many women, and what I had considered a useless time in my life was not useless at all.

Understanding that God can use even our past experiences is freeing—and scriptural. Paul says that God "chose us . . . before the creation of the world" (Ephesians 1:4) and that He "works out everything in conformity with the purpose of his will" (verse 11). How wonderful to know that God can blend the events in our lives with His purposes.

It might seem surprising, but many of us don't want to believe that God has a purpose in "everything." Granted, for some, the past is unusually painful, but we must be careful not to use unhappy times like an I.O.U. to claim that God owes us something because He "cheated" us when we were younger. I suppose many people would lose their excuses for self-pity if they released the hurts of the past. But there is no way for us to become the "new creatures" (II Corinthians 5:17) God intends if we don't let go of old hurts.

This principle is made clear over and over in Scripture. Isaiah, for example, speaks of it very directly in addressing the nation of Israel: "Forget the former things; do not dwell on the past" (Isaiah 43:18).

Hezekiah, after being healed by the hand of God and having fifteen years added to his life, saw the benefits of the chastisement he had suffered: "Surely it was for my benefit that I suffered such anguish" (Isaiah 38:17).

Also from the book of Isaiah comes this amazing picture:

"Woe to him who strives with his Maker, an earthen vessel with the potter! Does the clay say to him who fashions it, 'What are you making'? or 'Your work has no handles'?" (Isaiah 45:9, RSV).

The parallel is clear. God is the Potter and I am like the questioning pot when I refuse to accept either of the first two keys: God's love or my past.

There is a third key: Learn to be renewed.

Even when the distorting mirrors are put away, there will very likely be days of depression or discouragement. There is a "syndrome" at work here: guilt, followed by low self-esteem and then depression. Guilt is the major cause of low self-esteem and, among the women Dr. James Dobson surveyed for his book, *What Wives Wish Their Husbands Knew About Women,* low self-esteem is the major cause of depression.[2] You can keep guilt from sneaking in by a good "renewal" system.

Think of self-image—your true, heart-felt attitude about yourself—as the hub of a wheel (see diagram). The areas of your life that contribute to a sense of self-worth—like your physical appearance and your health—are like the spokes. If any one of these areas is out of balance, guilt can attack—often at a subconscious level. As this guilt attacks the self-image, it begins to produce stress and makes coping difficult.

For instance, when my house is clean, my weight under control and my relationship with my husband good, then I feel good about myself and my self-esteem is high. On the other hand, if my children are out of control, the sink filled with dirty dishes and I am two days overdue for a shampoo, my self-image is low and I tend to be depressed.

It is easy for us to try to live up to certain false standards and find ourselves ridden with guilt. In my early Christian life I believed the "spiritual" role to be more important than my duties as a homemaker. I thought that "putting God first" meant doing the spiritual not the practical things. So, dishes went unwashed and beds unmade while I spent hours counseling.

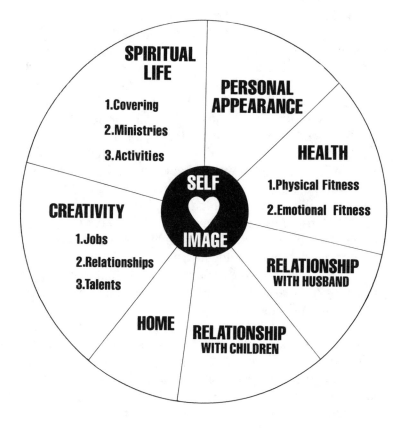

Meals were prepared in a rush so I could hurry off to women's fellowship meetings. Then, to compensate for guilt, I put more time and effort into religious activities when scrubbing the kitchen floor would have given me a more godly balance. God wants us to be balanced in body, mind and spirit.

The wheel illustration helped me realize something else. If you have ever ridden on a tire that had a rupture, you might remember that just before the bang came several seconds of a rough, uneven ride and an unusual thumping noise. In a similar way, there are warning signs like this in our lives.

As I look back I can see that when my life-wheel was well-balanced, my self-esteem was high and I was able to cope with all sorts of situations in a calm, efficient manner, however when it tilted out of balance, guilt hindered a good self-image and I was easily upset by the minor irritations of everyday life.

When I did not heed this first warning, I grew unhappy and I experienced outbursts of anger that surprised me as much as those around me. Then the depression would hit. Now I know I was failing to heed the warning signs of the guilt, low esteem, depression syndrome.

It would be wise for anyone reading this book to make a check list of personal strengths and weaknesses. Then, when you begin to notice warning signals, you can pour more of your energy into the *weak* areas and perhaps avert the guilt, poor self-image and resultant depression.

Every woman's life-wheel is unique and is continually changing. Among the myriad factors that affect it are marital status, the number and ages of children, God-given talents and the efficiency with which those talents are used.

Also, the importance given to different areas will vary according to current needs. Three of my four children are now away from home attending college so I have a great deal of time to spend in creative pursuits and spiritual activities. My friend Carol, on the other hand, is a gifted counselor, but spends the majority of her time at home with three children under age four. She currently has a very time-consuming role in her home, and, conversely, less time for counseling, recreation or creative pursuits.

Even though some roles receive greater focus than others, we still need to take part in *all* of them. I need to spend time in my home and Carol needs to pursue her spiritual growth. Then as the roles change, we simply flow with the new demands. Neglecting or resenting the current roles in our lives would throw off our inner balance and harm our self-image.

In the center of the life-wheel is the heart, the hub. In your own heart is the fourth key: Watch for the forces that motivate you. For those whose motives are wrong, even a balanced life will never run smoothly.

For example, our motive in serving God—whether in a supermarket, home or church—should be the love of people and the desire to see them set free, not to receive applause. A friend of mine discovered that her motive for disciplining her son was fear—fear that he would embarrass her in front of her friends.

Only if our hearts are set on pleasing God alone can our motives be pure. Since most of us have been conditioned from childhood to be men-pleasers rather than God-pleasers, it is hard for us to purify our motives. Yet, that conflict, trying to meet the world's standards rather than God's, can produce the guilt that leads to the same unhappy syndrome.

When all of the four keys are in operation, be careful about the fifth and final one: Don't get caught in the trap of perfectionism. Don't, in other words, allow pride to creep in with the thought that you can achieve far beyond your capabilities. Perfectionists consistently set goals that are beyond their abilities to achieve. Concentrate more on keeping your life in balance, running smoothly, with your thoughts and motives set on pleasing God.

Like other women I had to give up the idea of becoming

Wonder Woman and realize I was flesh and blood. I found that I, like Eve, had believed the serpent when he whispered, "You [can] be like God" (Genesis 3:4). In his book, *Come to the Party,* Karl Olsson emphasizes this: "I think death means climbing down from the perch of holiness, piety, self-denial, or whatever form the delusion that we can be superhuman takes, and simply accepting our humanity."[3] We can learn to live within the limitations of that humanity instead of above them; to set goals that are realistic rather than unreachable; to rejoice, not in strengths, but in weaknesses, knowing that it is in these very weaknesses "that Christ's power may rest on [us]" (II Corinthians 12:9).

As we discuss various roles in the succeeding chapters, ask God to show you your weaknesses and to give you both the desire and the grace to strengthen them. In my search, I found that balance and wholeness are obtainable, but I had to face some very honest revelations of myself. Seeing how we really are, without even the cover of a fig leaf, can be both painful and humorous. However, facing ourselves is a huge step toward freedom.

References for Chapter 3:

1. Dr. James Dobson, *Hide or Seek* (Fleming H. Revell Company, Old Tappan, New Jersey, 1974) p. 148.

2. Dr. James Dobson, *What Wives Wish Their Husbands Knew About Women* (Tyndale House Publisher, Inc., Wheaton, Illinois, 1975) p. 22.

3. Karl A. Olsson, *Come to the Party* (Word Books, Waco, Texas, 1972) p. 162.

4

Liking How You Look

I had been going to the same beauty shop every six weeks for about three years. Mary, my regular operator, was an ordinary girl with light brown hair and plain freckled face who, despite clever use of cosmetics, would never have turned heads in a crowd. She was transferred to another shop for a year and, when she returned, she had a different look about her. There was an inner glow that comes only to those love has touched.

After two visits, curiosity overtook my reluctance to meddle and I asked her, "Mary, what's happened to you?"

The glow became even more noticeable as Mary replied in a quiet voice that for the first time in her life she had found a living Christian faith.

Amazing! Faith did what no amount of cosmetics and grooming were able to do: Mary was beautiful!

As I sat there, my head covered with perm rods, trying not to breathe in the awful smell, I remembered a similar transformation in my life the day I turned forty.

I awoke that morning with the thought, *You are forty years old today,* foremost on my mind. About midway through the day, I stopped to freshen up my lipstick and comb my hair. As I bent closer to the mirror, I seemed to see myself with new eyes. It was almost as if a blurry image had finally come into focus. A thought startled me: *I like the way I look.* I had never felt that way about my appearance. Usually when I looked in a mirror I saw the hair that was out of place, the wrinkles beginning at the corners of my eyes, or some other slight or imagined imperfection. It seemed to me that God Himself had given me a birthday present. It may have taken forty years, but I finally liked and *accepted* my appearance.

It is not at all uncommon to dislike something about our physical appearances. Every woman I have ever talked to has rejected some aspect of herself: "My hips are too wide." "My breasts are too small." "My hair is too thin." "My nose is too large." Most of us measure ourselves against the *retouched* photos of Hollywood glamour girls and find ourselves short-changed. And no wonder.

To begin with, girl children are most frequently judged on the basis of appearance, ("My, what a pretty little girl"). Boys, on the other hand, are more likely to be judged on the basis of physical prowess, ("Let's see who can run the fastest"). Children's fairy tales emphasize the importance of beauty by picturing the princess as having a flawless complexion, lovely blue eyes, long blond hair—and she gets the prince plus a castle on a cloud. The villain is always described as dark and ugly, and comes to no good end.

Television commercials also do their part to maintain the fiction that beauty is the outward symbol of goodness as well as "forever after" happiness.

Earlier I mentioned that the Mirror of the Past had planted the suspicion that I was a bad child. My physical appearance did nothing to allay my fears: I wore glasses, braces and orthopedic shoes. To make matters worse, my dark hair was poker straight. If bad was related to ugly, I figured I didn't stand a chance.

Several years later the glasses, braces and orthopedic shoes were no longer needed and my hair had been permed in the latest fashion, but the ugly image remained. It was indelibly stamped on my spirit and even the new image in the mirror could not dispel the image of the past within me.

A good portion of my life was spent trying to improve my self-image by improving my appearance. I was the perfect sucker for every cosmetic ad that promised "younger looking skin," "wild, seductive eyes," "and deliciously, wicked lips." I exercised to keep my weight under control, fought cellulite relentlessly, steamed my face to restore lost moisture, colored my hair so cleverly that "only my hairdresser knew for sure" and elevated my feet once a day to promote circulation for good skin tone. Every new cosmetic, fashionable hairstyle, fad diet or up-to-date outfit held with it the promise that *now* I would really like the way I looked. It never worked.

Since I was convinced that my appearance was crucially important to my self-image, it is no wonder that I became ensnared by this same deception even in Christianity. I interpreted the Biblical injunction, "Do not be conformed to this world," as applying almost exclusively to one's appearance. The remainder of this verse makes it clear that we are to allow our thought patterns to change: then we are transformed from the inside out. I overlooked that and was misled into thinking that the only way to true spirituality was in changing my outward appearance.

The churches I attended had helped lead me into thinking that the more spiritual the woman, the plainer her appearance. Since my heart's desire was to be a spiritual woman, I set out to become as plain as possible. Fearing that the shock of becoming a spiritual giant overnight would be more than my system—and my husband—could bear, I decided to become plain in stages.

I began by overhauling my wardrobe, filling a Goodwill bag with my more "worldly-looking" garments. Later I decided it wouldn't really be good will to let other women wear the clothes that I considered to be an occasion of sin—so I stuffed them in the bottom of a large plastic bag and poured very wet garbage on top, hoping to make them unfit for human use.

Next to go were my earrings, for I had become convinced that pierced ears were a sign of "worldliness." About the time I reached this decision, I heard the garbage truck turning in at our street. Quickly scooping up all of my earrings, many of them 18 carat gold, I rushed out to the street, just in time to throw them on the truck. That dramatic gesture made me feel that I was well on my way to true spirituality. But for weeks I suffered a twinge of envy when I looked at my friends who were not yet convinced about the worldliness of *their* gold earrings!

It was several weeks before I got up the courage to deal with the matter of makeup. Like all women who consider themselves ugly, I had never dared to appear in public without "putting on my face." Gradually, very gradually, I began to wear less and less make-up. The time finally arrived when I went to the grocery store as barefaced as the day I was born. All the way there and back I was praying that I wouldn't meet anyone I knew, but deep in my proud heart was the conviction that I was truly spiritual.

The final step was the hardest. My hair had begun to turn gray while I was still in high school, and for years I had been coloring it. Being "convicted" that this was a deceptive practice, I finally decided that I would have to let my hair return to its natural color. I had been speaking before church groups regularly, and one imaginary scene kept returning. There I was, sharing what God had done in my life. Suddenly a man would jump up, point his finger at me and exclaim, "She has dyed hair!" Faces would stare at me horrified. The audacity to be a witness for Christ while my hair was proclaiming me a hypocrite! Yes, I knew I would have to return to my natural, God-given, but *blah* color. After many hair-cuts and one full year of having a two-tone head, my hair finally returned to the color God and age had made it. The sudden rise to such spiritual heights left me slightly giddy.

Before I could fully adjust to such a rarefied spiritual atmosphere, my husband decided enough was enough. One morning as I stood in front of the bathroom mirror washing my face, and reminding myself of the importance of sacrificing commercial beauty techniques, John came up behind me. He looked from my reflection in the mirror to the back of my head and announced, "I don't care for the natural color of your hair. I want you to color it again."

What a perplexing situation! I was just learning that a wife is supposed to submit to her husband, and here mine was ordering me to do something clearly contrary to the will of God.

Thank the Lord that He speaks to women through their husbands. John's intervention helped me to see that I had fallen into an age-old trap: overconcern with outward appearance. I thought that if I looked spiritual I'd be spiritual. A wise prophet said, thousands of years ago, "Man looks at the outward appearance, but the Lord looks at the heart" (I Samuel 16:7). I had been so concerned about how I looked to others that I hadn't let God deal with the real problem area—my heart.

As I began to return to a more normal style of dress and make-up, I realized that my efforts to look prim and proper had been robbing me of my spontaneity and joy in the Lord. I had actually been playing a role to make myself look the part of a Christian woman. As a result, I was beginning to take on the appearance of someone baptized in vinegar.

Much of the confusion in the Christian church on the subject of personal appearance has arisen, I believe, because of a misinterpretation of Peter's advice to wives. I Peter 3:3-4 says "Your beauty should not come from outward adornment, such as braided hair and the wearing of gold jewelry and fine clothes. Instead, it should be that of your inner self, the unfading beauty of a gentle and quiet spirit, which is of great worth in God's sight."

The Amplified Bible clarifies the meaning of this passage by inserting an important word, *merely:* "Let not yours be the (merely) external adorning. . . ." I don't believe Peter meant that women shouldn't wear fine clothing and otherwise make themselves attractive, but we should be more concerned with the attitude of our hearts than with the adorning of our persons.

Another scripture makes it clear that it is part of the wife's responsibility to clothe herself attractively. The perfect wife described in Proverbs 31 wears clothing made of "*fine* linen and purple" (verse 22, italics added). Both the material and the color are symbolic of festivity. Contrast these garments with the drab black and gray clothing so many religious groups want their women to wear.

Esther, in the Old Testament, had to complete a full twelve months of beauty treatments before she could even go into the king's presence (Esther 2:12). Shouldn't we, who are the bride of the King of kings also be concerned about our appearance and the preservation of His great gift to us—our femininity? It is that femininity which calls forth a man's protective and chivalrous nature. In today's society, women are taught to either ignore that part of their nature by the unisex look or emphasize their *femaleness* at the expense of their *femininity*.

My daughter and I witnessed this one night while watching a country music awards program on television. One after another of the female singers came to receive their awards with their high, bouffant hairdos. Their heads looked many times the normal size because of the teasing, and stiff from heavy doses of hair spray. The clothes they wore—tight fitting, electric colored shirts and jeans, or low cut, frilly dresses—added to the sense of unreality and gave the impression that they were giant, life-sized Barbie dolls. What a valuable object lesson for my daughter on the world's devices to make women appear foolish and unattractive.

Christian women should not be snared by the world's value system of appearance, but we do need to be concerned about how we look for a number of reasons.

First, the Bible says that we Christians are representatives of Christ (II Corinthians 5:20). This being the case, the world's judgment of Jesus is going to be based in large measure on the way His followers behave *and* on the way we look. At the time I was a new Christian, with my "religious" look, my sister, who was still trying to discover a faith of her own, would look at me and think, *If that's what its like to be a Christian, I don't want any part of it*. All she could see was that I looked like a frump and acted like a self-righteous boor. No wonder she wouldn't listen to my witness of the "joy" to be found in Christ.

Second, every marriage, including every Christian marriage, is in jeopardy today. If a woman becomes unattractive to her husband, she has weakened the foundation of that marriage. The wife who keeps herself looking nice in private as well as in public is telling her husband without words that she loves him and considers him important. The Bible tells us that "the woman is the glory of man" (I Corinthians 11:7), so how we look directly reflects on our husbands. Many times, a bitter, rebellious wife who is too "religious" to admit her feelings toward her husband, will neglect herself and therefore diminish her husband's "glory."

Third, a Christian woman with a poor self-image is both unhappy and ineffective. A good self-image is very dependent upon personal appearance. It is impossible for a woman to like herself when she is overweight, when her hair is in need of grooming, or when her clothes are unbecoming or need cleaning. If a woman becomes careless about her looks, this will establish an unhappy circle in which poor grooming leads to feelings of dissatisfaction and guilt, which in turn establishes even more slovenly patterns of dress, behavior and thought. The woman who knows she is looking her best will like herself better.

Ultimately, happiness does not come from what we look like on the outside, but rather, what we are on the inside. Jesus, who is to be our example, was probably not the strikingly handsome man he is so often pictured to be. Scripture says, "He had no beauty or majesty to attract us to him, nothing in his appearance that we should desire him" (Isaiah 53:2).

Apparently the Messiah was a very ordinary looking man who did not stand out from the crowd. For the first thirty years of His life, He attracted no particular attention. Then suddenly, He was the center of the most powerful ministry the world has ever known. No wonder the Jews said: "He's no better than we are. He's just a carpenter, Mary's boy, and brother of James and Joseph, Judas and Simon" (Mark 6:3, LB).

Even after He had been preaching, healing the sick, and performing unheard-of miracles for three years, Judas had to identify His Master by a sign: "The one I kiss is the man; arrest him" (Matthew 26:48). Jesus blended so well into the crowd that his betrayer had to point him out.

If one of our modern reporters were to cover the ministry of Jesus in today's setting, the account would be quite different. He would describe in detail the appearance of Jesus with, I am sure, special reference to His eyes. We would be told what He wore, how He walked and what He ate for His customary two daily meals. God, however, tells us about the character of Jesus. In Matthew, Mark, Luke and John, we learn how He reacted to various situations, the words He spoke which revealed His true nature, and His compassion for people. God is not interested in our duplicating Jesus' appearance, only His character. It takes a change in nature, not in appearance alone, for real happiness.

Even though we can all give assent to that truth, it was gratifying to hear one of the world's most beautiful women attest to it herself. I had clicked on the television set in the bedroom to keep me company while I stripped our bed of sheets. As the picture came into focus, the screen was filled with the stunning beauty of a famous television star. She delights in telling her age because people find it so hard to believe she is forty years old.

She was answering questions from the audience and their faces were as astounded and disbelieving as mine when she admitted that, until a year before, she had thought herself ugly.

The television host, usually quick with retorts, was likewise speechless. After a long moment, he asked in disbelief, "How could *you* think you were ugly?"

"Because," she replied, "I knew what I was like on the inside, and it was ugly."

The audience was dumbstruck. But I knew what she meant. I knew what it was like to feel horribly ugly, and I knew what it was like to release those depressing thoughts, accept myself, and learn to be happy with who I am.

Sometimes, we can gauge how we feel about ourselves by how we react to our physical appearances. In our home we have large mirrors on the closet near the front door. When I am at peace with God and myself, the image I see in the mirror is pleasing to me, even though I may have been too rushed to spend much time in personal grooming before going out. On the other hand, no matter how much time I spend on myself, I will not like my reflection if I do not have God's peace in my heart. God's peace comes from being obedient to God's will. "The unfading beauty of a gentle and quiet spirit" is not only "of great worth in God's sight" it is also more effective than "outward adornment . . . and fine clothes" in making a woman precious to her husband and to the other important people in her life. When "the inner self" of a woman is adorned with such a spirit, the outward appearance of that woman will be that of a worthy and winsome ambassador for Christ.

5

Shaping Up

Patrice had a not uncommon problem. No matter how tired she was, she couldn't sleep at night. And since her mind would not shut down when she climbed into bed, she tossed and turned and spent the night rehashing the problems of the day. By morning, she had worked even minor difficulties into unconquerable mountains, and as a result of the tension she was suffering intense pain from a spastic stomach muscle.

As we sat and talked, I tried to think of a scriptural principle that would help her out of her problem. I was stuck. Oddly, the only thing that came to mind was that she ought to start jogging, yet I knew about her total aversion to any type of exercise. She often stated that she was the most unathletic person God had ever created.

At the risk of sounding silly or simplistic, I finally said, "You know Patrice, you really ought to start jogging."

Surprisingly, Patrice responded with interest. She knew I had been jogging for about eleven years and I often touted its many benefits. Encouraged by her response I expanded on my suggestion, and explained that like other first-born children, she had a high motivation to achieve. But because she couldn't reach the level of achievement she desired, frustration built up and had no outlet. Jogging would be a good way to work off that excess energy.

Patrice went out and bought a pair of good athletic shoes and within two weeks the pain under her diaphragm was gone and she was sleeping soundly at night. "To get physically tired," says world-famous physician Dr. Paul Dudley White, "is the best antidote for tension."[1]

Patrice was so excited about the benefits of jogging that during her pregnancy she ran until the sixth month. She said she wanted the baby to have a relaxed and happy mother. An improved self-image was a fringe benefit that Patrice discovered by pushing herself to her fullest potential.

Patrice's experience serves to illustrate the delicate balance between our "ecological system" of spirit, soul and body. The proper functioning of one is dependent on the proper functioning of the other two. An over-emphasis in the spiritual area can lead to asceticism or occultism. A wrong emphasis on the "soulish" components (mind, emotions and will) can lead to unbalanced intellectualism, emotional instability or psychosis. Too much attention to the body can lead to narcissism, hypochondriasis or a fanatical interest in physical development. By the same token, *neglect* of any of these areas can also lead to serious problems.

God's plan includes wholeness in every area of life. Yet, as Christians, we often emphasize the spirit at the expense of the soul and body. Since the three are inseparable until death, we cannot neglect any one and have a balanced life. The apostle Paul wrote: "May the God of peace himself sanctify you *wholly;* and may your *spirit* and *soul* and *body* be kept sound and blameless at the coming of our Lord Jesus Christ" (I Thessalonians 5:23, RSV, italics added).

Why is physical fitness important? Medical considerations aside, the Bible commands us to glorify God through the body, which "is a temple of the Holy Spirit, who is in you" (I Corinthians 6:19). Stewardship applies to more than money; we are also stewards of the bodies God has given us.

In Old Testament times, the Jews considered their nation disgraced when the temple of God lay in shambles. They made every effort to restore it at the earliest possible moment so that the Shekinah glory of God would return to it (Ezra 3). Likewise, we must take care not to allow our bodies, the temples of the Holy Spirit, to become shabby, flabby and totally unattractive.

Keeping the temple of the body in top condition not only helps to glorify God, it also improves our efficiency, and therefore our self-image and sense of well-being. Unhampered by self-consciousness, inferiority or guilt, we are more likely to be instruments fit to reach the potential God has put within us.

Sometimes skeptics think of Christians as people so weak and spineless that they need their religion as a "crutch." This view is given credibility when Christians are so busy edifying their spirits that they neglect their bodies and their minds.

Paul, spiritual giant though he was, did not neglect his body, he disciplined it. He wrote, "Every athlete exercises self-control in *all* things. . . . I pommel my body and subdue it, lest after preaching to others I myself should be disqualified" (I Corinthians 9:25, 27, RSV, italics added). Paul recognized that the spirit should dictate to the body, not the other way around. A Christian who does not discipline his body is likely to be spiritually and emotionally undisciplined as well.

While volumes have been written and spoken about the importance of discipline in the spiritual activities—prayer life, Bible study and fellowship—very little has been said about discipline of the Christian's body. Yet that is often the part through which we represent Christianity. It is almost as if the body were too carnal a subject to be mentioned among Christians. But Paul, as we have seen, did not hesitate to talk about physical discipline; nor did he shy away from such carnal subjects as eating and drinking: "So whether you eat or drink, or whatever you do, do it all for the glory of God. (I Corinthians 10:31).

Lack of discipline in eating is certainly not glorifying to God, and gives offense to many. When my sister, Jeannie, was a new Christian, she became very irritated with overweight Christians who chided her about her smoking. Unbelievers often don't take Christians seriously who denounce drinking, smoking and even make-up, but glibly indulge in gluttony, one of the seven deadly sins!

It is interesting that Paul stresses physical discipline to the Corinthian church—a church which he said was "not lacking in any *spiritual* gift" (I Corinthians 1:7, italics added). Perhaps the members of that church, too, were, to quote D. L. Moody, "so heavenly minded that they were no earthly good." We must take care that we do not neglect the natural and practical areas of our lives and become stumbling blocks to others.

With that in mind let's consider some excellent ways to keep in shape, starting with a favorite of many of us: jogging. According to Haydn Gilmore, author of *Jog For Your Life,* "there are at least seven million joggers in the United States."[2] Why the great popularity of jogging? First of all, it's easy to fit into your schedule. You can run any time of day or night when you have twenty or thirty minutes to spare. Second, it requires a minimal outlay of money. All you need is a good pair of shoes. Third, you can jog by yourself. You don't have to round up other people before you can get started.

When I began jogging eleven years ago, I was so self-conscious about my lack of style and grace that I only jogged at night. The first time I ran a little more than half a mile—and thought I was going to die. After jogging daily for two weeks however, I could run a half-mile comfortably. Within a month I could run a full mile, and now I jog four miles five times a week.

Let's face it, expending ourselves does require self-discipline. There are times I am curled up on the couch on a cold winter evening, sleepy and comfortable, and suddenly an inner nudge reminds me that I haven't run that day. Looking out the window at swirling snowflakes, I usually shudder and sink deeper into the couch. But then I remember my commitment to God and eventually force myself to go out and jog. I am always glad afterwards.

Scripture tells us that "all discipline for the moment seems not to be joyful, but sorrowful; yet to those who have been trained by it, afterwards it yields the peaceful fruit of right-eousness" (Hebrews 12:11, NAS). I never have to wait long for the peace—I always sleep soundly after an evening run.

Jogging, of course, is not the only way to keep fit. Walking is probably the best all around exercise. A friend of mine who was quite overweight decided to start walking every day in addition to dieting. Contrary to popular thought, exercise decreases rather than increases the appetite. She found that within a month she had not only lost a considerable amount of weight but had more energy than she had ever had on previous diets.

Both jogging and walking, along with cycling, swimming, rope-skipping and dance exercise, are aerobic exercises, that is, they improve the body's use of oxygen. Many leading nutritionists believe that aerobic exercises can actually raise your body's metabolic rate—the rate at which calories are burned up—and that the effect lasts long after the exercise is over. This process seems to prolong life and give protection against heart disease. The most important thing is to maintain continuous exercise for twenty to thirty minutes at a time at least four times a week to obtain the maximum benefits.

Cycling can be particularly enjoyable for busy mothers. You can purchase a special seat for your toddler and give him a cheerful outing while you exercise. Older children can accompany you on their two- or three-wheelers. You can even let your dog run beside you and get a lot of exercise in a short time. Incidentally, tricycles for adults are becoming increasingly popular. Some senior citizens in small communities use these grown up three-wheelers as their only means of transportation.

Another big benefit of an exercise program is the ability to make a commitment and stick to it. If you are the type to start projects with enthusiasm but never finish them, such a regime may be what you need to bring discipline to your life. Scripture tells us that "the spiritual did not come first, but the natural, and after that the spiritual" (I Corinthians 15:46). Disciplining the physical body translates into discipline of the soul and spirit.

There is another very important point to consider in this vital interrelationship of body, soul and spirit: It is quite possible that exercise could be a partial solution to emotional and mental problems.

Doctors feel that many disorders of the mind are caused when certain "stress" chemicals reach large levels in the brain. These chemicals are released to equip or "charge up" the body for "fight or flight." When the body remains inactive, however, the chemicals are not used up, and are released in large doses into the blood stream, and carried to the brain.

Early in my life, I developed a pattern of stomping off to bed when I encountered stress that I couldn't handle. Full of anger and frustration, I lay there brooding for hours. Then for days afterward I was depressed, sometimes to the point of being suicidal. All my brooding, combined with physical inactivity kept the harmful chemicals from being safely released, and built up a state of despair.

After I became a Christian, I realized that type of behavior was intolerable. In an effort to reverse all my learned patterns, I forced myself to respond differently to criticism or conflict. No longer did I allow myself to indulge in thoughts of anger or self-pity. On several occasions I reacted with my old habit of retreating to bed. But, as soon as I realized what I was doing, I made myself get up and resume my normal activities.

It was some time before I understood the importance of

exercise in relation to to my mental and emotional well-being. When I found my schedule overloaded, the first thing to go was exercise. I reasoned that taking care of my body was really selfish when I could be serving others.

Very soon after I stopped exercising, I would begin to experience depression. For some reason I never related the depression to inactivity. However, something dawned on me one day: The heavier my schedule, the more stress I am under. Since I don't handle stress very well, I need more, not less, physical exercise during busy times, to work off the effects of stress chemicals on my system. It's no wonder that, shortly after giving up physical activities, I would go into a chemically induced depression. Since I made this discovery, I have not experienced one period of depression, even though my schedule has become busier every year.

Exercise doesn't have to be work. It can be *fun* and can have benefits other than physical fitness, such as strengthening family ties.

The epigram, "The family that prays together stays together" has a rhyming corollary: "The family that *plays* together stays together." Parent-child participation in some game or recreational activity can fill the need for a physcial workout—and can do as much as anything I know to bridge the gap between generations, especially as children move into their teens.

When the whole family is united in the same activity, whether a parlor game, tennis, swimming, or walking in the woods, parents and children are, for once, all working toward the same goal. Sometimes that goal is simply to top each other; sometimes it is to reach a destination at the end of a hike or bicycle ride; sometimes it is to master a new skill. Often children can end up teaching and helping their parents.

My oldest son and I learned to water ski at the same time, and he proved to be much more proficient than I. We have both enjoyed his giving me pointers that have helped to improve my skill and enjoyment of the sport. Young children often feel that there is nothing they could ever do as well as their parents, and very little that they can do *for* their parents. Finding they can give their parents a helping hand greatly enhances their self-image, too.

Walking can be fun for the whole family, as well as helping us feel better about ourselves. Long before I became a Christian and learned to draw on that support, I decided to break my two-pack-a-day cigarette habit. Soon, the daily urge to smoke was fairly under control—until mid-afternoon. Then, when I became so desirous of a cigarette that I couldn't concentrate on anything else, I bundled up my three toddlers in their winter clothing—a job in itself—and took them for a long walk. By the time we returned home, I was calm and peaceful and free from the desire for a cigarette, and my three youngsters were tired and relaxed, ready to settle down to some quiet activity until dinner was on the table.

God has built into the world He created a natural tranquilizer—the beauty of the outdoors. Psychologists have found that the colors of nature are the most soothing colors to our spirits. If we mothers spent more time outside walking, working or playing with our children, we would, consequently, spend less time inside yelling at them. We might feel better about ourselves as mothers.

If it is important for parents and children to have fun together, it is equally important for *parents* to have fun together, just by themselves. A candlelit dinner for two, a game of tennis, or perhaps just an evening stroll can give a husband and wife the opportunity to renew their appreciation of each other and to reopen the channels of soul-to-soul communication that tend to become clogged by the daily trivia of family life.

Naturally, time together may be limited when the children are small, but later in life there comes a time when every wife has a choice. She can continue to confine her recreation to shopping trips and bridge games with her friends, or she can learn to enjoy whatever forms of recreation appeal most to her husband.

Too many women, as they grow older, are reluctant to learn new skills for fear of getting hurt or being inept and looking "silly." Rather than accompanying their husbands on fishing or golfing outings, they refrain from enjoying the leisure time that could be spent together. It may be difficult to learn to enjoy these new things, but it is rewarding.

About ten years ago, my husband decided that he wanted to try skiing. I was thirty-five years old and had never been on snow skis in my life. Besides that, because my feet had frozen when I was a child, I didn't like winter sports—and I had a terrible fear of heights. But I realized it was a question of learning to ski with John or staying at home alone. I chose skiing.

John and I went skiing twice a year, and for the first three years I never enjoyed a minute on the slopes—or even getting up the slopes. Riding the chair lift was sheer terror. Gradually, however, I became accustomed to swaying in a chair suspended high above the snow-covered terrain, and finally, with a tremendous feeling of accomplishment, I realized I had conquered my lifelong fear of heights.

That wasn't the end of my problems with skiing, however. Basically an insecure person, I have always liked to feel "in control." Being on unwieldy skis brought me face to face with insecurities I had skillfully buried.

Though I appeared to be making an effort to ski, inside I was uptight trying very hard to remain upright. At the end of a day of skiing I was completely exhausted—emotionally as well as physically. After about four days of that, I was a nervous wreck. I usually spent the last day of our five-day ski and "fun" package crying, sulking, and sometimes vomiting.

It was in our fourth year of skiing that my persistence was finally rewarded. On our first trip to the slopes that year, I found myself unaccountably relaxed. I was skiing just for the fun of it!

From that time on, our skiing trips have been enjoyable for both John and me, and I feel satisfaction from overcoming the crippling fear of insecurity.

As I look back now on those early miserable experiences, I thank God for them, and for making me a better person through them:

1. Waiting in long chairlift lines increased my patience.
2. Learning to ski just to have a good time helped me to unlearn some of the competitiveness I had acquired as a child.
3. Overcoming the fear of heights and the fear of losing control—not only of my equilibrium, but also of the circumstances of my life, and as a result of this lesson,
4. Trusting God to control *every* circumstance of my life, including releasing my husband and children to His care as never before.

Not wanting to face insecurities can make us afraid to venture out of the safety of our own little ruts. But if we remain in controlled and familiar environments, we lose in the long run by missing opportunities to grow and to feel better about ourselves.

Remember that no matter how fun or challenging the activity, rest is essential to maintaining the temple of the body in good condition. The leaning tower of Pisa is one of the seven wonders of the world precisely because it hasn't yet fallen, even though it is off balance. Few of us would be so fortunate!

Dr. Hans Selye, whose pioneer work on stress is discussed in Chapter 6, says that "All work and no play is certainly harmful for anyone at any age."[3] He suggests two rules to follow in order to prevent stress-induced disease.

The first is, "If there is proportionately too much stress in any one part, you need a diversion."

After several hours of intense mental effort, one needs to engage in some activity that will give her body exercise and set her brain free from the need to concentrate: a walk, bike ride or even cleaning the house will rid the brain of stress chemicals far more effectively than a nap.

His second rule is, "If there is too much stress in the body as a whole, you must rest." If fatigue is more physical than mental, then we need rest rather than just a change of pace. And don't forget the importance of observing Sunday as a day of rest. Scripture is very clear on that: "Six days you shall labor and do all your work, but the seventh day is a Sabbath to the Lord your God. On it you shall not do any work . . ." (Exodus 20:9-10). Whenever I disregard this commandment and allow Sunday to become another day of work (even work for the Lord), I feel the effects all week.

God wants His children to be in balance physically, mentally and spiritually. Paul says that the presentation of our bodies "as a living sacrifice to God" is our "*spiritual* worship" (Romans 12:1, italics added). How can our worship be pleasing to God if the body that we offer Him has been either neglected or pampered, underworked or overworked, starved or stuffed? Through balance achieved by discipline let us keep our bodies fit to be presented to God as a living sacrifice and as the dwelling place of His Spirit.

References for Chapter 5:

1. Richard Bauman, "The Ulcer Personality," *SKY,* (November 1980) pp. 70-72.
2. Haydn Gilmore, *Jog for Your Life,* (Zondervan, Grand Rapids, Michigan, 1974), p. 13.
3. Hans Selye, *The Stress of Life,* (McGraw-Hill Book Co., Revised Edition, 1976), pp. 413, 416.

6

Hidden Emotions

For the most part, our self-images are out of balance for obvious reasons. We don't like the way we look or how we cling to a bad habit. But sometimes the problem is rooted deep within us: We have become angry, depressed, resentful, unforgiving for reasons we don't understand. These hidden areas are part of emotional fitness that need to be brought into balance.

A number of years ago, my mother, sister and I were washing and drying the dishes after a "family get-together" dinner. The Sunday evening sounds of *Walt Disney* were coming from the living room. Our husbands and children were cast into a sleepy after-dinner trance from the feast of roast beef, Yorkshire pudding and Mom's delicious creamed spinach casserole. I was glad to hear my father's laughter mingled in with the others', since at the last big dinner he had been quiet and sullen. We knew he was upset but, as often happened, we didn't know why.

Mother changed the subject of our amiable threesome's conversation with the tone which usually heralded some portentous statement. "Well," she said, "I finally found out what was bothering your father."

Inexplicably, I felt an immediate tightening of my stomach

muscles. Before I could stop myself I snapped, "I don't want to hear it, Mother."

Paying no attention she launched into an explanation of my father's previous pointed silence. *Could she possibly imagine I was joking?* I thought, agitated. As she continued talking my hostility mounted. "I told you I don't want to hear it," I repeated, near tears, and appalled at the grating tone of my own voice. That time she heard me and stopped short as my sister regarded me in astonishment.

"What's the matter?" my mother asked, clearly puzzled.

"I'm sick and tired of your always putting Dad down."

Absolute silence.

Mother's mouth fell open and Jeannie stared blankly. Their obvious dismay made me realize that I was taking out on them some problem of my own. As quickly as it came, my anger subsided, leaving me confused. "Please," I said. "Could we sit down and talk about this?" I sent up a frantic prayer for wisdom.

As we sat around the table discussing my sudden volatile reaction, I began to see it reflected unresolved tensions from my childhood. The three of us doing dishes together again had triggered long-buried, almost forgotten emotions of a sensitive period in my life that had coincided with a strained time in my parents' marriage.

Although there was never overt hostility between them, I found myself trying to take both sides, my mother's because she was right—my mother, I thought, was always right—and my father's because I loved him anyway no matter how wrong he was. If Dad was late for dinner and Mother remarked that it was thoughtless of him, it hurt me. I made a hundred silent excuses to justify him in my heart. I was frustrated in my efforts to be peacemaker between them, for of course, a child trying to play this role among adults is hopelessly out of her depths.

The need to justify my father translated into a hidden resentment of my mother, who knew his weaknesses so well. I discovered, that Sunday night, that the key word is *hidden*. I never felt any conscious animosity toward my mother. Quite the contrary. We had the normal mother-daughter conflicts as I was growing up, but I felt that the majority of these were my fault and often marvelled at her patience with her "difficult" daughter. I idealized her as the perfect mother and wife. If anyone had told me I had hatred in my heart toward her, I would have denied it vehemently.

But God knew. And He used that flare-up on a seemingly amiable Sunday evening to show me my need to forgive. Then and there I confessed my resentment, hatred and judgment of my mother during that period of our lives and, as the Disney seranade faded out in the living room beyond, we hugged and cried together.

No wonder Paul Tournier, noted Swiss physician, laments that there is very little forgiveness going on at a deep level. I could see that most of the forgiveness I had experienced as a new Christian had been shallow and superficial. I had never before obeyed the command of Jesus to "forgive from your heart" (Matthew 18:35).

Before giving that command, Jesus answered Peter's question about forgiveness by telling a parable. Most of us are familiar with the parable of the forgiven, then unforgiving servant in Matthew 18:21-35, but we generally pass over the punishment meted out by the Master.

> Then the angry king sent the man to the *torture chamber* until he had paid every last penny due. So shall my heavenly Father do to you if you refuse to truly forgive your brothers.
> (Matthew 18:34, LB, italics added)

> And his master, in anger, gave him over to be *tortured* until the debt was paid.
> (Matthew 18:34, Knox, italics added)

What might the "torture chamber" represent to us? Perhaps
we can include the physical and psychological effects of resentment, bitterness and anger. Doctors today are becoming more
and more conscious of stress-induced diseases. Some experts
believe that as much as ninety percent of all illness is psycho-
genic—that is, the result of mental or emotional conflicts. The
psychological torture that a person endures when he begins to
hate can also affect his bodily functions; the subconscious mind
can actually weaken the body's resistance to disease. In discussing the "high cost of getting even," a medical doctor writes:

> The moment I start hating a man, I become his
> slave. I can't enjoy my work any more because he even
> controls my thoughts. My resentments produce too
> many stress hormones in my body and I become
> fatigued after only a few hours of work.[1]

The body responds to the emotions of hate and resentment
just as it does to cold and fatigue, except that the stress produced
by emotional factors seems to be even more harmful than that
due to physical causes.

Dr. Selye used the following diagram to illustrate the body's
reaction to stress:

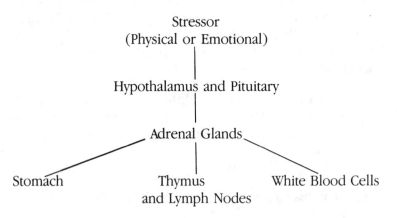

Stressor
(Physical or Emotional)

Hypothalamus and Pituitary

Adrenal Glands

Stomach   Thymus   White Blood Cells
            and Lymph Nodes

I was particularly interested in the important role played by the adrenal glands in stress reaction. The adrenals are small glands buried in the fat on top of the kidneys. The hormones secreted by these glands stimulate all other organs and glands.

In the Old Testament books of Exodus and Leviticus, God lists the kidneys (translated *reins* in the King James Version), along with other organs of sacrificial animals, to be given as offerings. The Hebrews considered the kidneys and heart to be the centers of the emotions and the will. In each of His directives to them about sacrifices (Exodus 29:13, 22; Leviticus 3:4, 10, 15; 4:9) God specifies the "two kidneys with the *fat* that is on them"; remember it is in the fat that the adrenal gland is located. Burning these organs upon the altar symbolized the offering up of man's will and emotions to the control of God.

What this says to me is that thousands of years before scientists recognized the harmful effects of stress, godly men of the Old Testament repeatedly emphasized the importance of letting God control our emotions. Jeremiah, in talking about the wicked, said to God: "Thou art near in their mouth and far from their *reins**" (Jeremiah 12:2). In other words, the people he referred to said all the rights things, but their emotions and wills were not under God's control. Sometimes a person who is constantly praising and thanking God verbally is doing so in an effort to convince himself and others that buried hostilities aren't really there.

In Psalm 16:7 David said, "I will bless the Lord, who hath given me counsel: my *reins* also instruct me in the night seasons." *The Modern Language Bible* says, "I will bless the Lord who has counseled me; even in the night my *emotions* admonish me."

How do our emotions admonish us "even in the night"? Among the signs of stress listed by Dr. Selye are insomnia,

---

* *Here and elsewhere throughout these quotations, italics have been added and all quotations are from the KJV.*

bruxism (teeth grinding, which is most common in sleep), and nightmares.[2] When our emotions keep us from having a peaceful night's sleep, they are telling us that something is wrong. Among the emotions that the Hebrews ascribed to the reins were *joy,* "Yea, my *reins* shall rejoice when thy lips speak right things" (Proverbs 23:16); *sorrow,* "Thus my heart was grieved, and I was pricked in my *reins*" (Psalm 73:21); and *desire,* "Whom I shall see for myself, and mine eyes shall behold, and not another; though my *reins* be consumed within me" (Job 19:27).

God is called the searcher of the *reins* as well as the heart (Psalm 7:9; 26:2). To Jeremiah He said, "I the Lord search the heart, I try the *reins,* even to give every man according to his ways, and according to the fruit of his doings" (Jeremiah 17:10). As this scripture indicates, we truly do reap what we sow. If we have sown discord, bitterness and unforgiveness, our own bodies will pronounce judgment upon us and produce physical as well as mental torment.

If resentment and bitterness become habitual, the resulting stress will eventually take its toll on our bodies. As Cecil Osborne explains:

> Man is body, mind and spirit, and what affects one affects all. If there are inner conflicts and tensions, anxiety and guilt at some point in his life, the individual will tend to manifest this spiritual dis-ease by some physical symptom. If he does not, his dis-ease may take the form of psychic masochism, an unconscious need to punish himself. He may become accident prone . . . or bad-judgment prone.[3]

Many respected Christian leaders today teach that healing will come to anyone who claims it with sufficient faith. They base this teaching on the premise that it is never God's will for one of His children to be sick, and on scriptures such as Isaiah 53:5:

"Upon him was the chastisement that made us whole, and with his stripes we are healed" (RSV).

For the most part, I agree with this premise. Certainly it is not God's will for a man to make himself sick by harboring hatred and bitterness. But *claiming* a healing is not the answer. Since according to estimates, ninety percent of all illness is *emotionally induced,* we must first let God take care of the emotional factors causing the illness.

Even if God saw fit to honor faith by giving supernatural healing of an ulcer, for example, the relief would be only temporary unless the victim got rid of the harmful emotions which caused the ulcer. If he remains tense and anxious or bitter and unforgiving, whether toward himself or toward someone else, those emotions might sooner or later lead to some other illness . . . arthritis, perhaps. Eventually he will have to deal with the real issue: the sin in his life.

Consider the case of Norman Cousins, editor of *The Saturday Review,* who had a miraculous recovery from a fatal collagen illness.[4]

Since he was given very little hope of recovery according to traditional methods of treatment, he decided to become his own doctor. He moved out of his hospital room to a hotel room which provided a more serene environment. He began to watch amusing movies and found that ten minutes of genuine belly laughter had an anesthetic effect and gave him at least two hours of pain-free sleep. He seemed to prove the physiologic basis for the proverb that "a cheerful heart is good medicine" (Proverbs 17:22).

He reasoned that if negative emotions produced negative chemical changes in the body, then positive emotions should produce positive changes. He felt that love, hope, laughter and the will to live would have therapeutic value.

Today, he is totally pain free and each year his mobility has improved. He is living proof that the will to live is a physiologic reality.

Studies indicate that it is not the stress of life that destroys us but rather our *response* to that stress. Some time ago, I was counseling Gwen, a middle-aged mother of three teenagers, about her children. In the course of the conversation, she shared something that seems to reinforce this statement.

Gwen was only a sophomore in high school when her mother suffered a nervous breakdown and had to be hospitalized indefinitely. Since she was the only girl still at home, she had to quit school and stay home to care for her father and brothers. Even though she had to make sacrifices, Gwen was never resentful. She considered it a part of her responsibility to her family.

Her brother, Mike, on the other hand, responded just the opposite. When he was forced to drop out of college and work to help pay medical expenses, he became bitter and claimed that his mother had ruined his life.

Today, Gwen's brother is a diagnosed schizophrenic and has spent the majority of his life in institutions. Mike viewed himself as a helpless victim: a pawn in the game of life, at the whim and mercy of a capricious God. Gwen, who accepted what happened to her without blaming anyone, without resentment or self-pity, has had a happy and fulfilled life. Isn't it amazing how the same environment can produce two such different responses?

As Christians, we should never consider ourselves helpless and hopeless victims. First, we have Jesus Christ within us, who, Scripture says, is our "hope of glory" (Colossians 1:27). The book of Romans also tells us that "in this hope we were saved," and, "if we hope for what we do not yet have, we wait for it patiently" (Romans 8:24-25). Paul then describes how the Holy Spirit Himself will help us in our weakness (verse 26).

Second, no matter what circumstances come to us in life that seem beyond our control, we *can* control our attitude, our response to the situation. If we respond in anger, resentment and self-pity, the resulting stress will begin its destructive work in our lives. If we set our wills to accept and rejoice, we will never be defeated by circumstances.

Third, if we have given God control of our lives, then we have to believe that "in all things God works for the good of those who love him, who have been called according to His purpose" (Romans 8:28).

We are never helpless victims of circumstances but we, with the help of God's grace, are always in control of our responses. Those responses may very well determine the quality and length of our lives.

No wonder Jesus constantly admonished His followers to forgive, to "love your enemies and pray for those who persecute you" (Matthew 5:44). He knew what it costs to be unloving. Not only does resentment and hostility rob us of the righteousness, peace and joy that are our inheritance as children of God, the stress produced by those emotions will eventually take its toll. In essence, we will have committed *ourselves* to the torture chamber. And we not only hurt ourselves, we cause pain to those around us.

Young women should be aware, for instance, of the evidence that stress during pregnancy has adverse physical and even mental effects on the fetus. This phenomenon has been called the "syndrome of transmission." According to Dr. Selye, "There is good evidence that exposure of pregnant women to un-usually severe stressors may cause developmental anomalies and malformations in their fetuses, even if it does not lead to abortion.[5] Proverbs 23:7 says, "For as he thinketh in his heart, so is he" (KJV). Perhaps we should add this corollary: "As a *woman* thinketh in her heart, so is her unborn child."

The medical profession has recognized for some time that the woman who smokes, drinks alcoholic beverages or takes certain drugs during pregnancy is endangering her baby's health and perhaps his life. Babies can even become addicted to alcohol and drugs in the womb.

God, being aware of the "syndrome of transmission" long before Dr. Selye demonstrated it, warned Samson's mother to "drink no wine or strong drink, and eat nothing unclean" while she carried her child, because he was to "be a Nazarite to God from birth" (Judges 13:4-5, KJV). A Nazarite was one who took certain strict vows—among them, never to cut his hair or drink strong drink. Apparently, because of the syndrome of transmission, Samson could not have been a Nazarite "from birth" if his mother had failed to observe these vows.

If alcohol and drugs can affect our unborn children so easily, imagine the impact of negative emotions such as bitterness and rejection on the developing fetus.

Other results of unhealthy emotions are not as obvious. For instance, neither I nor those around me were aware of one of the effects my sense of failure was having on me. I was going so far as to drum up recurrent illness, subconsciously, to avoid facing failure. This revelation came some years ago, when my husband and I were to host a large dinner party. The day before, I came down with severe bronchitis. Naturally the party had to be cancelled.

As I was lying miserably in my steam-fogged room, I asked God why it was that I got sick whenever I had a lot to do. I seemed to hear a very clear answer: "Because you want to escape." My eyes flew open at the impact of those words—but deep down inside I acknowledged that they were true. I was suddenly aware that throughout my life I had followed a pattern of escape, chiefly because I always seemed to be rewarded for being ill.

When I was sick as a child, I could stay home from school while my mother waited on me hand and foot. Having a tonsilectomy was even pleasant, since it meant presents, extra attention and as much ice cream as I wanted.

A high school incident further promoted the idea of illness as an escape. I had such a burning desire to be a cheerleader, that in my junior year I finally mustered up my courage and entered the tryouts.

To my surprise, I made it through all the eliminations right up to the finals. Having watched the other girls perform, however, I knew deep in my heart that I wasn't quite good enough to be chosen. So, I was faced with a dilemma: If I competed in the finals and was eliminated, I would have to face the fact that I had failed. If I didn't compete, I would feel like a failure for quitting. Failure was something I just couldn't handle.

The dilemma was conveniently solved when I came down with a very high fever the day before the finals. The examining doctor found that I had *two* punctured eardrums. Physical activity was out for a few days.

I can still remember my thoughts that day as I lay in bed picturing the tryouts that were then taking place. I knew I had found the perfect cop-out. I pretended to be disappointed, but deep down I was gloating. It was easy to play the role of the magnanimous loser when I went back to school and my friends said, "What a rotten break! We *know* you would have made the squad. This lesson in escape was imprinted indelibly on my subconscious mind, and served me in college with another big payoff.

Being a very competitive biology major in a very competitive pre-medical school, the stress was beginning to take its toll on me. One night just before exams began, I woke up in a state of panic, sweating and gasping for breath. My roommate called the paramedics, who administered oxygen, and recommended I see a doctor for tranquilizers. My family doctor diagnosed my condition as a severe anxiety reaction, and advised bedrest.

Because I was a straight-A student, every one of my teachers excused me from his examination and let me keep an A in the course. What a reward for being sick! There I was, lounging in bed, reading magazines and watching television while my class-mates were sweating out final exams.

For months after that, I had frequent returns of that terrible, suffocating feeling of anxiety, but the habit of escape through illness was too deeply ingrained to be laid aside.

With marriage and the birth of my first child, I felt so insecure and inadequate that I actually welcomed the numerous sick-nesses,even major operatons,that plagued my life for a number of years. The pain was a relatively small price to pay for several weeks of relief from responsibility and for receiving the tender loving care of my friends and family as further compensation.

The day before the ill-fated dinner party, when I finally real-ized the self-deception, I wanted to be whole. I no longer wanted to escape from the stress of life, but to learn to work through it.

For the next few months, I fought quite a battle, as the symptoms of every illness from bronchitis to kidney infections threatened to lay me low. Each time I began to feel sick, I would quietly pray, "Lord, I don't want to escape. I want to do every-thing You have for me to do." Amazingly, within a day or two the symptoms would disappear and I would feel great.

The hardest part of the lesson was realizing that I didn't want to face my need to escape because it reflected my unforgiving nature; I simply refused to acknowledge the existence of un-acceptable emotions. The desire to escape my responsibilities was unacceptable to me; so I buried it deep in my heart (or "reins"), where it could do its dirty work unhindered by my conscious will.

Now, when someone "hurts my feelings" or otherwise of-fends me, I pray and ask the Lord's help in forgiving the other person for the offense, and myself for being resentful. One of the quickest ways to improve your self-image, I have found, is through forgiveness of others. As I learn to accept and forgive others, I am learning to accept and forgive myself, weaknesses and all.

I say *amen* to Dr. Selye's statement that "it is well worth the effort and humiliation [to learn to know yourself] because most of our tensions and frustrations stem from compulsive needs to act the role of someone we are not."[6]

If we can learn to forgive others *and* ourselves as freely as God forgives us, we will escape the torture chamber created by emotional stress, and become the balanced people we want to be.

References for Chapter 6:

1. S. I. McMillen: *None of These Diseases,* (Fleming H. Revell Company, Old Tappan, New Jersey, 1974), p. 72.

2. Hans Selye: *The Stress of Life,* (McGraw-Hill Book Co., revised edition, 1976), pp. 175, 177.

3. Cecil Osborne: *The Art of Understanding Yourself,* (Zondervan Publishing House, Grand Rapids, Michigan, 1967), p. 47.

4. Norman Cousins: "Anatomy of An Illness," *Reader's Digest,* (June 1977), pp. 130-134.

5. Hans Selye: p. 275.

6. Ibid., p. 405.

7

Two People, One Flesh?

Some time ago, Ann Landers conducted a survey among her readers. The question was asked: "If you had it to do over again, would you marry the person to whom you are now married?"[1] Within 10 days she received 50,000 replies—fifty-two percent voted "No." Unfortunately, many unhappy marriage partners are taking action. Statistically, one in every two marriages ends in divorce, with the divorce rate among Christians closely paralleling the world's statistics.

Many marriage counselors blame the unprecedented rise of divorce on the "me decade" or the "new narcissism" of this age. One counselor stated that the question often running through the marriage is, "Hey, is this jerk I married fulfilling me?" Instead of looking into ourselves to find the reasons for unhappiness, we are more likely to shuck our partner and look for fulfillment with someone else.

An ambitious woman who desires a Christian ministry sometimes feels that her partner is keeping her from serving God. It is not uncommon for a wife to feel she is the more spiritual of the twosome and the "plodder" she married as a weight around her neck.

This type of thinking results from failure to understand the concept of becoming "one flesh" (Genesis 2:24). To be one flesh means to be one in body, soul and spirit. Although a newly-wedded couple may be thinking only of the physical union, God has much more in mind. After the wedding vows, God no longer sees two separate individuals, but one; marriage is a merging of two distinct identities into one complete whole. The lighting of one unity candle from two candles during many wedding services is symbolic of this union.

For the two to become one in every area means dying to individual opinions, rights, egos and desires. This is a lifelong—and necessary—process. Jesus said, "unless a kernel of wheat falls to the ground and dies, it remains only a single seed," (John 12:24) and we will remain single individuals rather than be the one flesh God intends unless we, too, are willing to "die" to ourselves.

When talking about the marriage relationship in Ephesians 5:22-33, Paul said, "This is a profound mystery—but I am talking about Christ and the church." Somehow, the marriage union is analogous to our union with Christ. Just as we have to surrender our wills so that Christ might live in us, so in marriage we must surrender our wills to bring that union into fulfillment.

Certainly a woman begins her marriage "in love" with her husband. She is usually attracted to him because his personality traits appeal to her, complement her own demeanor, or perhaps because his personality is the exact opposite of hers. Why, then, do many women begin to complain about those very traits that seemed attractive? Why do so many of us try to make our husbands over to be more like *us* rather than appreciating the God-given differences?

Some psychologists believe that a simple, unconscious jealousy may be behind these complaints. When I met my husband in college, I was at the height of my struggle to prove myself academically. I was immediately attracted by his relaxed attitude about life. Grades didn't seem to matter to John, and studying was definitely not his number one priority. After we were married, it was that same happy-go-lucky quality which bothered me most about my husband. I was always nagging him to be more disciplined. Not understanding the one flesh concept, I saw him as a competitor rather than a complement to me. Naturally, the more I criticized him, the more he had to defend his way of doing things and the further away we moved from each other. I'm sure I was subconsciously yearning to be as free from concern as he was, but I couldn't let go of my standards.

That struggle to hold on to what I thought I should be led to a conflict within me—actually a paradox. I was afraid to give in and lose my identity, yet, I was frustrated all the while at not being able to *find* it. When John and I finally became "one flesh" my image became completely melded with his, and I had new avenues of fulfillment. The idea of becoming "one flesh" can be a bit frightening, but that is only until you discover the joy and boost to your self-image of being one with your husband and as you discover the right way to "submit" to your husband.

I had been a Christian only about a year when I learned there were actually courses on submission. I took all the courses I could and read all of the many books I found on the subject. Although I never seemed to master the idea of submission in my heart, I *acted* submissive, hoping that somehow, some day, my heart would come into line.

One Wednesday evening, as I was watching my husband lead a prayer meeting in our home, I began to feel deeply uneasy about my heart's attitude. I sat there looking spiritual, but my heart was filled with criticism and judgment against my husband for the way he was conducting the meeting. Over and against these criticisms came the thought, like a clear-sounding bell, that I was *one flesh* with my husband. In criticizing John, I was destroying my own flesh. I recalled, too, a Bible verse, Proverbs 14:1 (RSV): "Wisdom builds her house, but folly with her own hands tears it down" (RSV).

That night it became plain to me that, although I had submitted to John in a legalistic way, true submission was something more; my heart had to be right. And when I got honest with myself, I saw the true reason why I did not respect my husband's spiritual authority: *pride*—pride in the spiritual gifts God had graciously bestowed upon me. Like so many women, I had begun to think my gifts were a sign that God "approved" of me, proof of my spirituality. In so thinking I had come to consider my ideas and ways of doing things to be superior to John's.

After having the true condition of my heart exposed to me that night I could retain no false illusions about my spirituality. Right then and there I made up my mind to submit in my heart to the wonderful man God had given me. With that resolve, I began noticing many ways in which I had shown disrespect without even being aware of it. For instance, I often made jokes about John in front of the children. "Of course, I'm only teasing you," I would always add, but the children got the message that Dad wasn't quite as competent as Mother.

One day about six months after my resolve—we were in the midst of family prayer—a thought hit me: My husband was a completely changed person! Gradually, so gradually that I hadn't even noticed it before, he had assumed the full spiritual headship in our family. When I recognized his position as head of the household, his spiritual stature increased until his authority rested on him easily.

I then saw that his practical, easy-going nature was the perfect complement to my impulsive, idealistic character. I would jump feet first into something, realize it was the wrong way to go, and try to find a way out. John, on the other hand, was deliberate and thoughtful, a trait I had previously criticized as "dull." He "counted the cost" before he made a decision. As a result, the commitments he made were sure and he was faithful to them. As I saw my need for his wisdom, I naturally moved closer to him. Then he could lay down his defenses and move toward me, for he was no longer threatened that I would flag our differences. As we moved closer together into that "oneness" God intended, I realized more and more what a perfect complement we were to one another—almost like two interlocking jigsaw pieces. His strengths fit perfectly into my weaknesses and my strengths into his weaknesses.

Many a Christian woman reacts negatively to God's command to *submit* to her husband. Perhaps they overlook the statement Paul adds, "And the wife must *respect* her husband" (Ephesians 5:33, italics added). Without respect submission means nothing.

One of David's wives, Michal, the daughter of Saul, failed to respect her husband. In fact, as she watched David "leaping and dancing before the Lord, she *despised* him in her heart" (II Samuel 6:16, italics added).

God's judgment on Michal was swift and hard: "And Michal the daughter of Saul had no child to the day of her death" (II Samuel 6:23). In Old Testament times children were considered a sign of God's blessing; barrenness brought shame and disgrace to a Hebrew woman. God took away from Michal the very thing that made her particularly a woman. Many women today who lose their femininity may lose it for the same reason Michal lost hers: they despise their husbands.

God's viewpoint on this has not changed over the three thousand years since the judgment on Michal. God's Word *commands* the wife to respect her husband; the woman who fails to do so is breaking a law of God which carries a penalty. She loses her joy in the Lord, and her face soon reflects the bitterness and resentment in her heart. Worst of all, her children will grow up like their mother, not respecting authority and ultimately causing heartbreak to both parents. Difficult as it may be at the time, it is always better to obey God.

Learning godly respect is only the first step toward oneness with your husband. Abigail, another woman of the Old Testament, gives an excellent example of intercession on our husband's behalf.

Unlike Michal, Abigail had good reason to despise her husband, Nabal. We learn in I Samuel 25:3 that Nabal, although a man of great wealth, was "surly and mean" while Abigail was described as "intelligent and beautiful."

When David was being pursued by Saul, he sent word to Nabal that he and his men were in need of provisions. It was well known that David was the king ordained by God and that it was just a matter of time before he would begin to rule. Nabal, however, pretended to have no idea who David was, and responded to his request with typical churlishness:

> Who is this David? Who is this son of Jesse? Many servants are breaking away from their masters these days. Why should I take my bread and water, and the meat I have slaughtered for my shearers, and give it to men coming from who knows where?
>
> (I Samuel 25:10-11)

Angered by this insult, David decided to take revenge. When Abigail received a report of the incident and of David's plan, she promptly gathered a generous load of food supplies and took them to David. Falling at his feet, she said, "Upon me alone, my lord, be the guilt. . ." (I Samuel 25:24, RSV).

Abigail is a model of how a wife should serve as an intercessor for her husband. If a man does something that calls for God's judgment, his wife should intercede for him in prayer. I believe this is one of the most important ministries a wife can undertake. Sadly, too many wives today are eagerly awaiting God's judgment upon their husbands so that they can smugly say, "I told you so."

Abigail so identified with Nabal that she could say to David, "Pray forgive the trespass of your handmaid" (I Samuel 25:28 RSV). Being a woman of "intelligence," she understood the concept of becoming one flesh with her husband and knew that *what affected him would affect her.* Therefore she became an intercessor and stood in the gap, as the prophet puts it (Ezekiel 22:30), between her husband and the king's judgment.

David was so moved by this humble woman's plea that he blessed the Lord for sending her and blessed her for the "discretion" by which she had saved him from an impulsive and foolish act. When Abigail returned home that evening, Nabal was throwing a party and was disgustingly drunk with wine. Therefore she waited until morning to tell him what had transpired.

How different she was from most of us wives! If ever I did anything as noble and successful as Abigail I probably would announce it publicly to the whole feasting crowd. I would never have the self-control to wait until morning. But she did, and when Nabal was sober, she told him what she had done. Immediately Nabal suffered what appears to be a stroke. The Bible says, "His heart failed him, and he became like a stone. About ten days later, the Lord struck Nabal and he died."

Notice the Bible says that *God* struck Nabal. God foresaw that Nabal was a man unwilling to change, no matter how godly the behavior of his wife. God Himself avenged the wrong done to his anointed, David, and set Abigail free from an impossible situation. Notice, too, that *God* set Abigail free; she made no effort to gain her own freedom.

Although this is an extreme example, the principle holds in many situations: God will deal with the husband only when the wife is in her proper place and has the right attitude. God uses difficult situations to mold us into the image of His Son, and He will not remove the difficulties until they have done their work of developing in us the character qualities He desires. Many women make the best of an unpleasant situation, but they do it with a martyr-like attitude which robs them of the good God intended to bring out of that situation.

Other women try to use submission as a technique to serve their own purposes, and get upset when God won't cooperate with them and change their husbands. Much of what has been taught about submission is simply a manipulative, subtle effort to control the other person. Manipulation is just one step away from witchcraft—a spiritual ritual to gain one's own ends—which God says is an abomination to Him.

God has summed up the principle of submission in Philippians 2:3-4, not only for wives, but for all who would call themselves followers of Christ. "Do nothing out of selfish ambition or vain conceit, but in humility *consider others better than yourselves.* Each of you should look not only to your own interests, but also to the interests of others" (italics added). If we would truly count others *better than ourselves* we would naturally be submissive and respectful. If we do not, Paul says it is because of our "selfish ambition" or "vain conceit."

The wife who will honor her husband and give up her desires in order to see him successful is fulfilling the third step of becoming one with her husband: She is presenting a beautiful picture of Jesus to her children. We know that a child's first concept of God is derived from his parents. It has been widely accepted that the child's father represents God the Father, and the child's attitude toward his earthly father will eventually be directed toward God. Every mother should consider how she can represent Jesus Christ to her child. Just as Jesus did not "seek his own will, but only the will of his Father" (John 5:30), so the wife who is submissive to her husband's authority is representing Christ to her children. What a beautiful, balanced picture of God: two separate persons, yet one flesh; two different aspects of God, yet one God.

When we can put these steps into action, we no longer fear the thought of losing our identities. When we are willing to follow God's leading, we will find His plan for our lives and be fulfilled.

The results of this are wonderful. Almost at once, John and I began to find a deep intimate relationship on the soul level.

Many Christian couples achieve *physical* and *spiritual* unity—
for two partners who are both born-again believers in Jesus
Christ *are* one in spirit. Relatively few marriage partners, however, become one at the *soul* level. The soul is composed of the
mind, the will and the emotions. Only when there is a deep
level of mutual trust are two people able to yield their minds,
wills and emotions to each other for the purpose of being made
one.

Moving into this oneness on the soul level is a difficult
process, because it means uncovering your thoughts, feelings
and inner desires. The scriptural statement that "the man and
his wife were both naked, and they felt no shame" (Genesis
2:25), refers, in my thinking, to more than physical nakedness.
For the typical woman brought up in this "enlightened" era, it is
much easier to undress in front of her husband than to uncover
her dark thoughts and emotions before him, exposing the
ugliness that sometimes lies within her human soul. And yet, it
is only after a husband and wife expose those shadowed areas to
each other that God's light can drive out the darkness, freeing
them and bringing them into beautiful unity with each other
and fellowship with Him. As the apostle wrote:

> If we claim to have fellowship with him yet walk in
> the darkness, we lie and do not live by the truth. But if
> we walk in the light, as he is in the light, we have
> fellowship with one another, and the blood of Jesus,
> His Son, purifies us from every sin.
>
> (I John 1:6-7)

John and I soon learned that we would be unsettled with the
children, with friends, or at work if there was any unresolved
conflict or misunderstanding between us. We had to learn to be
completely honest about our feelings toward each other; we
couldn't hold hurts or resentments inside. To be less than

completely honest resulted in a break in our fellowship—and until that was mended, neither of us had any peace. But this was a big barrier to overcome, and it took time.

Like so many women, I had longed for years for that intimate relationship with my husband on the soul level. However, John was reared in a home where his parents did little if any communicating, and then it was usually through loud arguments. Try as I would, I could never get him to open his feelings to me at a deep level. I soon learned that this was not unusual. In fact, as I began to read books, studies and articles by counselling experts, a pattern emerged.

Most marriages, it seems, flounder for a lack of good communication. Sadly, a study shows that the average couple spends a mere ten minutes a day in conversation. The majority of wives feel it is their husbands who are uncommunicative and emotionally reserved. Yet, other statistics seem to belie that charge. At least half of all husbands are unfaithful, and the reason, according to Reverend Peter Kreitler, marriage counselor and author of *Affair Prevention,* is a longing for closeness, kindness and togetherness; a need to feel appreciated.[2] In fact, the women to whom these men turn describe them as extravagantly emotional, seemingly starved for intimacy.

Ironically, Dr. David Reed, former associate director of the Marriage Council of Philadelphia, says that "women's innate and enormous ability to love frightens men into withholding their feelings in order not to lose control. They sense that more is expected of them than they have to give."[3] Many men are uncomfortable with intimacy because they see the relationship as yet another competitive struggle that they could very well lose by giving in to their feelings and making themselves vulnerable. Those same men do not have the competitive feelings with a casual lover that they have with their wives, and this gives them a freedom to share.

As I read these unhappy reports, I came to see that respect

and submission, which God has commanded, are the way to gain a man's trust. This is vitally important before he can feel the freedom to share his deepest thoughts and feelings.

Yet, it appears that most of us women want to extract trust out of our husbands without having established a solid base, forgetting that men have certain emotional orientations just as we do.

A husband can trust his wife because he knows she will never use his weaknesses to belittle or ridicule him in front of sympathetic friends. I am appalled at the freedom with which some women speak of their husbands' faults with other women. They would be thoroughly shocked if their husbands were equally frank with colleagues at the office about *their* shortcomings. The type of loyalty and discretion displayed by the Proverbs 31 wife is sadly lacking in most women.

The intimacy we women yearn for with our husbands may be unrealistic if we believe the feminist philosophy, that the only difference between men and women is sexual. Even feminists are starting to complain about the effects of such thinking. Betty Friedan recently wrote "There don't seem to be any men."[4] As my husband and I counsel young Christian couples, we find that one major complaint of the women is a lack of sexual desire on the part of their husbands.

This is certainly a reversal of sexual roles. In trying to obliterate the distinction between the sexes, we have lost that distinctly masculine quality which women desire in their men—and there is "compelling evidence" that men, too, need to have the difference between the sexes clearly defined,[5] starting at a very early age.

A baby boy must at some time turn away from his mother to find himself. He needs to turn toward images of maleness that are powerful enough to compensate for his mother's enormous attraction over him. The boy's father should fill this role, but in our society the father is often absent or too unsure of his own identity to pass his maleness along to his son.

Annie Gottlieb, the author of this theory, suggests that "men need to reenact the separation from the mother again and again" and this need will be directed toward their wives.[6] Since a woman's first experience of intimacy is with her mother, a woman can remain intimate without diminishing her femininity. Men on the other hand need to get away into the world of work, sports and other men to re-establish their masculinity.

I had a chance to share this information with Nicole, a young Christian woman who came to see me about her marital problems. She reluctantly confessed that after being married only two years, their sex life was practically non-existent. Her husband was an active Christian worker and spent quite a bit of time away from home, ministering. "When he is home," she tearfully admitted, "he is always too tired to spend any time with me."

We talked about how her demands for intimacy, both conversationally and sexually, could be driving her husband away from home. She understood that he wasn't rejecting her personally, but the motherly, domineering figure she represented.

I was pleasantly surprised to hear from her just two days after our talk. When she was no longer threatened by his desire to achieve, but saw it as a need to establish his masculine identity, she was able to release him, not just with words but with her heart. He, in turn, became less defensive about his activities outside the home and responded by being more sensitive and loving to her.

We women seem to change from girl friends to mothers the day we say, "I do" and even more so after the birth of the first child. But no man wants another mother, usually the one he has is more than he can handle. Nagging will only deteriorate a relationship—either by arguing or withdrawing on his part. We must abandon the desire to "mother" our husbands and remember that we were called to be helpmates, completers, co-regents in a kingdom that is definitely not matriarchal.

Recent research reveals another barrier to relating intimately at the "soul" level: Differing brain functions give women an advantage in verbal communication. According to Dr. Richard M. Restak, a neurologist, "each hemisphere is specialized for a different cognitive style."[7] The left hemisphere of the brain works in an "analytical" mode, a logical approach in which words are ideal tools, while the right hemisphere favors a visual-spatial mode, a clearer view of the overall picture. Women draw on the left "verbal" hemisphere, while men learn not so much by hearing and talking as by doing.

From birth, female infants are more sensitive to sounds, tones of voice and intensity of expression. They speak sooner, possess larger vocabularies and very seldom demonstrate speech defects.

Boys, on the other hand, are more curious about exploring their environment. They want to take things apart to see how they work. They are curious about what goes in to making a "whole," and are often bored, such as in classrooms where girls shine, to sit and listen to explanations. They want to see things for themselves, and often pursue professions such as architecture and mathematics, making excellent use of their developed right hemispheres.

Since women are better verbal communicators, it is easy to see why most men shy away from us when we want to "sit down and *talk* it over." They are at a competitive—not to mention biological—disadvantage. It would be hard to number the times I've heard a man say, "I can never win an argument with my wife."

Does this mean we have to forego a deep level of communication? Not at all. Men want and need to communicate feelings and desires, but have often felt inadequate and frustrated trying to do so. This is another important reason to build trust in our husbands, so that they will be able to learn to communicate and express themselves freely.

Understanding the differences in brain function reinforces

the idea that husbands and wives are only complete when we are one flesh. Although men can see the overall picture, they need us women to fill in the details. They may see the forest, but we see the individual trees, which is why women are more sensitive to people and their needs.

John and I see the world differently. Yet, our combined view is so much broader than my narrow incomplete picture. This has been a great boost for my self-image, since I am not losing my identity but gaining a new one—broader, deeper and more complete than anything I could have on my own.

I know that my husband and I have just begun to discover the full implications of what it means to be one flesh. But in this discovery God has given us a small taste of the joy and blessing to be derived from bringing two lives into one under the Lordship of Jesus Christ.

References for Chapter 7:

1. Ann Landers, "If You Had It To Do All Over Again, Would You Marry The Same Person?" *Family Circle,* (July 26, 1977), pp. 2, 52 & 54.

2. Judith Jobin, "Why Husbands Stray And How To Make Them Stay," *Woman's Day,* (February 8, 1983), pp. 20-24.

3. Maxine Schnall, "How to Sensitize The Insensitive Man," *Woman's Day,* (February 5, 1978), pp. 38, 40, 42 & 90.

4. Annie Gottlieb, "What Men Need That Women Can't Give Them," *McCall's,* (October 1983), pp. 103, 166, 168 & 170.

5. Ibid.

6. Ibid.

7. Richard M. Restak, M.D., *The Brain: The Last Frontier,* (Doubleday & Company, Inc., Garden City, New York, 1979), p. 176.

8

Self-Image and Children

A mother's self-image is inextricably bound to her children. It is almost impossible for a woman to feel good about herself if she thinks she has failed as a mother, because our children are, in a very real sense, extensions of ourselves, reflecting both our good and our bad qualities.

All of us have at one time or another felt overwhelmed by the demands of parenthood. As Christians, we face the added concern of raising children who are not only successful in their careers and social lives, but also godly. This pressure can lead to breakdowns in communication between husbands and wives. In fact, studies show that "a couple's satisfaction with marriage and with each other drops sharply soon after their first child is born."[1] This is not what God intended. He said children were to be a blessing (Psalms 127:3) not a burden.

Yet, a mother with a poor self-image does feel burdened—even threatened—by her children. She needs constant encouragement that she is doing the right thing.

There is a big reason we react so strongly to the weaknesses in our children: they are mirrors of our own weaknesses. I can remember listening to my children in the next room playing house and repeating my own words. It sounded very inappropriate to hear my four-year-old say, "Just shut up and do it because I said to."

Often, there will be reflections in our children that don't please us, but if we ask God for the grace to change those same areas in our own lives, children can become a blessing. In this way, we will be growing and changing along with our children and our self-image will improve because of these changes.

One problem that can affect self-image through our families is the lack of unity. Many parents feel that children have harmed their marriage, when, in truth, the children have only brought a marriage problem to the surface. Many couples unconsciously use a child as the battleground to discharge their anger at one another.

One couple in our Fellowship came for counselling one night about their youngest child, Joanne, a strong-willed little girl of seven who challenged every decision her parents made. After a brief discussion of their daughter's problems, the couple launched into a fiery argument with each other. It became clear that the child was caught in the power struggle over which parent would be disciplinarian. Aware of a real lack of authority the child ran from Mom to Dad creating bedlam. Even though she seemed to enjoy causing them to fight, she was filled with fear at the ease with which they were divided. She was infinitely more hurt by the lack of stability in her home than she would have been by a good spanking from her father. Until the couple was better able to communicate their differences they were not likely to see a change in Joanne.

Unity between parents is paramount in raising children. As mothers we seem to worry about each decision as if the child's whole future depended on our doing the psychologically correct thing at any particular time. We can follow all the books and theories and even back up every decision with Scripture, but we will still fail with our children unless we are one with our husbands in mind and heart. Long after a child forgets that he had to stay in his room all afternoon for lying or that he wasn't allowed candy an hour before dinner, he will remember whether he felt the security of his parents in agreement or whether "Dad said I had to, but Mom was on *my* side." The long-term result of parental unity will be self-confidence and self-discipline. But self-discipline will never come easy to someone who has experienced division between his first disciplinarians—particularly if the child is the battleground for working out the conflicts and resentments.

If we find ourselves arguing over the children frequently we should stop and ask the Holy Spirit to reveal the real problem. Perhaps we are hiding anger, hurt and disappointment with our mates or ourselves. The unity that we maintain will give our children the security they need to grow up strong and confident in this changing and frightening world. That unity will also add to our self-esteem because of the combined strength we give to one another.

The need for children, even adult children, to have this sense of security in the home was reinforced one weekend when my third child, Tom, came home to visit for several days. He is in his second year of college and going through that confusing time of goal setting, and trying to decide what he wants to do with his life. He stayed around the house most of the weekend—unusual for a young adult with his own car—and when he left on Sunday evening, he said he felt peace knowing things would work out for him.

Tom found peace in the security of his home environment. It was almost as if God said to him, "Look Tom, even though you are all confused and the future is vague and frightening, things at home are still the same; nothing has changed there." The home environment, especially the love between a husband and wife, should reflect the love of God to the child—committed, enduring, continuous. It is a reminder to the child of the unchanging nature of God.

Because our children read our heart-attitudes as well as our words, we can see that what *we* are will determine, to a great extent, what *they* are. Jesus, the Son of God, was "the image of the invisible God," His Father (Colossians 1:15). In the same way, our children are the "image" of us parents. My greatest motivation for getting my own life in order is to be able to be the kind of person I want to see reflected in my children.

It was years before I saw how my mother's poor self-image reflected in me. Mother was a kind, loving woman who believed her children could do anything and offered us a lot of positive reinforcement. Yet, even with her encouragement, I grew up with a negative image of myself. In the last few years, especially since the death of my father, I have seen that my mother is a very insecure person with deep feelings of unworthiness. In spite of her efforts to convince me I was a worthwhile person, she passed on to me her heart-attitude, and with it, her poor self-image.

When my oldest daughter, Shannon, was in the seventh grade, I realized that I had continued this "sin of the generations" and passed on my inner self-hate and worthlessness to her. She was hurrying to get ready for school one morning and couldn't get her hair to do what she wanted it to do. She was very emotional that day and just as I passed the bathroom, she pounded her reflection in the mirror and shouted "I hate you, I hate you."

I realized then, that all my words to encourage her were as useless as my mother's were with me. I needed to learn to love myself so that my daughter could learn to love herself. As I saw myself breaking bad habit patterns and bondages from the past, my self-image improved greatly knowing I was not going to leave the same legacy to my daughters. And I have seen the fruit in Shannon's life as well.

God's Word says we are to "*train* up a child in the way he should go, and when he is old he will not turn from it" (Proverbs 22:6). That word *train* implies more than just teaching the child God's precepts and commandments; it also suggests that we are to show by example—*our* example—what it means to walk in God's way.

It is useless to tell a child that God wants him to "turn the other cheek" if he sees us respond with anger when people mistreat us. How can we teach our children the importance of forgiveness when we nurse a grudge against our husbands for days? Of what value is it to tell your children to be kind and courteous if they see you give a tongue-lashing to an indifferent salesclerk? All our words, Bible studies and prayers with our children are wasted efforts if we don't apply Biblical principles in our daily lives. One frustrated teenager put it this way to her parents: "Don't keep preaching to me about Jesus and then keep living the way you do!"

This does not in any way minimize the importance of teaching our children the Word of God. God's commandment is clear:

> These commandments that I give you today are to be upon your hearts. Impress them on your children. Talk about them when you sit at home and when you walk along the road, when you lie down and when you get up.
>
> (Deuteronomy 6:6-7)

Sometimes women wonder how much, if any, responsibility they should assume for their children's spiritual nurture if the father is to be the head of the house. The answer is found in Proverbs 1:8: "Listen, my son, to your father's *instruction,* and do not forsake your mother's *teaching"* (italics added). The dictionary definition of *instruction* is "the act of furnishing with authoritative directions." The scriptural pattern, then, is for Dad to give the overall directions, while Mother teaches her children why they should obey their father.

This division of responsibility should work out well even for wives of non-Christian husbands. Suppose, for example, that a father told his son that he wanted him to take full charge of lawn maintenance. The mother could then teach her son from Scripture what God says about obeying and respecting one's parents (Exodus 20:12; Ephesians 6:1-3), about doing all things without murmuring and complaining (Philippians 2:14), and about sluggards (Proverbs 6:6,9; 10:26; 13:4; 20:4; 26:16). In teaching him that he should carry out his father's instructions with a willing and joyful heart, as serving God and not man (Ephesians 6:6), she would be showing him how to put basic scriptural principles into practice. I don't believe any father, Christian or non-Christian, would object to this type of Bible teaching for his son.

A mother cannot help teaching her children—if not by precept, then by example. If she has a poor self-image, she will take one of two stands: either she will not discipline her children for fear of losing their love, or she will become domineering in an effort to control their every action. We need to find the balance between discipline and love that springs from a good self-image. It helps to have some goals—to know some of the most important concepts a mother can teach her children.

Probably the most important principle we can teach our children is respect for authority. Many Christians have the mistaken belief that God commands us to respect only those authorities who, by virtue of their character, wisdom, and/or maturity, are worthy of respect. But the teaching of the Bible is that the authority invested in a person's *position* is distinct and separate from that person's *character:*

> Everyone must submit himself to the governing authorities, for there is no authority except that which God has established. . . . Consequently, he who rebels against the authority is rebelling against what God has instituted, and those who do so will bring judgment on themselves. For rulers hold no terror for those who do right, but for those who do wrong.
>
> (Romans 13:1-3)

Paul goes on to ask the question, "Do you want to be free from fear?" And his answer is simple: "Then do what is right." This same principle operates no matter who is in authority over us: father, mother, teacher, employer, supervisor or husband. If our conduct is right, we will live without anxiety; but if we are doing wrong—in deed, word or attitude—we will live in constant fear of incurring judgment.

Many theories on child-rearing are based on erroneous views of authority. Parent Effectiveness Training (P.E.T.) which was so widespread it was called by the *New York Times* "a national movement," is founded on the premise that the parent and child have equal rights, and that the parent therefore should not use his authority over a child.

This destructive theory and others have contributed to the newly discovered Battered Parent Syndrome. Parents are actually living in fear of physical abuse by their own children. According to Don Cuvo, a marriage-and-family therapist, the main reason for such abuse is lack of an authority structure. "Youngsters need firm structure. They may object verbally, but that's what they want. And parents aren't providing it."[2]

The principle of submission to authority must be *taught* to our children and then *demonstrated* by our lives. Because Jesus understood this principle, God was able to carry out through Him His plan for the redemption of mankind.

Instead of resisting the soldiers who came to arrest Him in the garden (Matthew 26:53), Jesus rebuked Peter for attempting to defend Him with the sword. In reply to Pilate's question, "Do you realize that I have power either to free you or to crucify you?" Jesus answered, "You would have no power over me if it were not given to you from above" (John 19:10-11). Jesus recognized that Pilate's authority could come only from His own Father, God.

David also understood this principle of submission to God's will. No wonder God said that David was a man after His own heart (I Samuel 13:14). Knowing that whatever happened to him in life was under God's control, David wasn't even worried about defending his reign when he was fleeing from his son Absalom: "If I find favor in the Lord's eyes, he will bring me back (to Jerusalem); . . . but if he says, 'I am not pleased with you,' then I am ready; let him do to me whatever seems good to him" (II Samuel 15:25-26).

If we can teach our children respect for authority, this will produce in them a submissive spirit, which is the direct opposite of the self-assertive spirit the world demands. This submissive spirit is the very spirit of Jesus Christ Himself which enabled Him to say: "I seek not my own will but the will of him who sent me". (John 5:30, RSV).

A mother with a poor self-image may have a difficult time taking her God-given authority over her children. First, she will not feel the authority she needs to stand firm in her directives, and second, she fears she will lose the love of her children if she tries to discipline them.

Having undisciplined children severely undermines a woman's sense of self-worth. How can she think much of herself when she can't even control her children? Just as the centurion in the Bible recognized that Jesus had His authority because He was under authority (Matthew 8:9), the mother also, receives her authority with the children because she is under her husband's authority. If she is truly in submission to her husband, the children will respect her and obey her decisions.

I have counseled many young married women who have had to forgive their mothers for not training and disciplining them when they were growing up. They came to realize that many of the struggles in their adult life could have been avoided if they had only been taught discipline.

Another important thing to remember is to "rejoice in the Lord *always*" (Philippians 4:4, italics added), regardless of outward circumstances. Christians talk a great deal today about being "children of the King." Harold Hill has coined the expression "King's kids" to emphasize our royal standing. We know that God wants only the best for His "kids," and some Christians jump to the conclusion that "the best" means nice houses, big cars and plenty of money. The Bible says, however, that "the Kingdom of God is not a matter of eating and drinking, but of righteousness, peace and joy in the Holy Spirit" (Romans 14:17).

Happiness, it is true, is dependent upon what is happening to us. Joy and peace, however, are attitudes of the heart which are not dependent on outward circumstances but on an inward assurance that our heavenly Father is in complete control of everything that happens in our lives. If parents could impart this assurance to their children at an early age, how much more stability their lives would have!

Unfortunately, attitudes of the heart cannot be taught, but can only be demonstrated. Therefore, if your children are to know the basis of true joy, watch how you respond to problems. This will let your children know whether you really believe that God is in control of your life. Are your children able to see that you "consider it pure joy . . . when you face trials of many kinds" (James 1:2)?

I always thought that in the face of big trials I would show my children how to meet them. I could picture myself calmly facing atomic warfare, floods, tornadoes, persecution—any trial God allowed to come my way. Finally, however, I realized that it is seldom through the major tragedies that our real character is disclosed, but in the everyday, petty irritations. And in these, I usually come through with less than flying colors.

I find it hard to "consider it pure joy" when the washing machine breaks down on Monday morning; when one of my children comes down with intestinal flu and I have to cancel a long-awaited luncheon engagement; when I am frantically trying to prepare a meal for unexpected guests and a child chooses that time to ask for help with his homework. My response in these situations reveals to my children whether my life is controlled by the Holy Spirit: a long freight train when I am in a hurry—I can practice patience; a dear friend hurts me—a chance to practice forgiveness; the sales girl ignores me—an opportunity to be humble. When I am flowing with the stream of the living God, allowing the power of the Holy Spirit to work in my life, I am making progress in my image of myself and how my children see me.

Once when my then thirteen-year-old son, Tom, and I had just been informed by a doctor that he needed surgery to correct a birth abnormality, the nurse who came in to set up a time for the operation was not only indifferent to our feelings but was actually rude. In answer to a quick prayer, I felt the Lord's love for her, and was able to answer her graciously. After she left the room my son told me the thought of surgery didn't frighten him so much, since I was so calm and peaceful.

We saw that same nurse many times after that, and she was never rude to us again. In fact, she often went out of her way to accommodate us.

It it is probably safe to say that no class of human beings feels as guilty as mothers today. Because no responsibility is greater than giving life, mothering and guilt are often intertwined. We feel responsible if our children are ill, if they are handicapped, if they fail a test, lack a date to the prom or get a bad case of acne. Mother is the favorite scapegoat of psychologists and comedians.

Perhaps it is because of the overwhelming guilt that mothers are abdicating their positions in the home in unprecedented numbers today. According to a firm that locates missing persons, a record number of mothers will leave home this year—more mothers than fathers.[3]

I can remember different periods in my life, especially when I had four teenagers in the house, that I felt overwhelmed at the guilt of having failed. We all go through times when we see no redeeming qualities in our children and are sure we have totally botched the job of mothering. Several days later we may wonder how we could ever have felt that way about such wonderful human beings.

To maintain the positive self-image that our Father wants all his children to have, we mothers need to see ourselves and the job of mothering as God sees it. He has entrusted our children to us for the few short formation years, but in reality they are not ours at all. They are His. We have a very important, even formidable, task to do; yet the final responsibility He keeps for Himself, their growth, their lives, their salvation. That is why we should constantly practice (and it does take practice!) releasing our children to God from the moment they are born.

Once I realized that human effort will always fall far short of the heavenly goal, I no longer felt guilty. Instead I was washed in a great sense of relief that I couldn't carry the burden of the children myself. That release has been tested by more than one incident of adolescent rebellion, but I know, that in spite of outward circumstances, God is in control of my children's lives and He will continue to help them grow in His grace until His task within them is finally finished (see Philippians 1:6).

The book of James tells us that "we all stumble in many ways" but God's Word also says that "love covers over a multitude of sins" (I Peter 4:8). I can rest knowing that, although I may have made many mistakes in rearing my children, I did love them and acted on what I perceived to be the right thing at that time.

I have to trust in God's grace to make up what is lacking in my efforts. There is a paradox in Christian mothering. We are to work as hard as we can to raise godly children and, at the same time, realize all our efforts are in vain if God is not in control of our lives and our children's lives. Someone has said we are to work as if everything depended on us and pray as if everything depended on God. This is the perfect formula for the Christian life, but especially for the high calling of motherhood.

References for Chapter 8:

1. Marcia Lasswell and Norman Lobsenz: "How Children Can Hurt A Marriage," *McCall's,* (September 1977), pp 161, 200, 202, 204 & 206.
2. Cliff Yudell: "I'm Afraid of My Own Child," *Reader's Digest,* (August 1983), pp. 78-82.
3. Gerri Hirshey: "When Mommy Leaves Home," *Family Circle,* (August 23, 1977), pp. 70, 72, 74 & 76.

9

The Challenge of Homemaking

Jesus, speaking of His life on earth, said to His followers, "Foxes have holes and birds of the air have nests, but the Son of Man has no place to lay his head" (Matthew 8:20). Implicit in this remark is the recognition that having a home meets one of the deepest needs of the whole animal kingdom. The home as God intended it to be is a place of nurturing and activity, laughter and security, a reflection of heaven, which is to be our lasting home.

The most successful millionaire or the brightest achiever who lives in a house filled with resentment and anger would gladly change places with a less gifted person who can count on a warm welcoming smile. Jesus knew this truth when He told His disciples, "In my Father's house are many rooms; if it were not so, I would have told you. I am going there to prepare a place for you" (John 14:2). They received comfort at the prospect of a happy, eternal homecoming.

If a home is so important in the full development of human potential, then it seems a homemaker would have a high level of self-esteem. Instead the belief prevails that it is impossible for an intelligent woman to find fulfillment in her home, and anyone who does must be afraid of challenge or excitement in her life. The modern American housewife is generally pictured as neurotic: bored, depressed or anxious. "Psychologists and sociologists study her in interviews and surveys, and conclude, in Jessie Bernard's words, 'Being a housewife makes women sick.'"[1]

Homemaking *is* a trying profession, but not because it lacks challenge. Just the opposite is true: homemaking is a life of constant responsibility. The old adage, "a man may work from sun to sun, but a woman's work is never done," is all too true for the homemaker who is constantly in her "work" environment. She can't cover the typewriter and close the office door on her work-day, so the distinction between work and nonwork blurs. It is also hard to see tangible rewards since the same chores need to be done day after day without the benefit of a paycheck for her efforts. She may also be isolated from people, especially if she has young children.

The world's view has certainly added to the poor self-esteem of many housewives. The women's liberation movement was given great impetus by the publication of Betty Friedan's best-seller, *The Feminine Mystique*. In this book she went to great lengths to prove that repetitive household chores are a waste of an intelligent woman's skills and education. In a recent article, however, she writes about her love for cooking and admits that she has missed practicing this domestic skill.

This puts Friedan in something of a predicament: She has publicly rejected household chores as drudgery, now she wants to justify taking some of them up again. Her article ends with a statement which undoubtedly raised some eyebrows among her fellow women's libbers: "I think now that I will cook when I feel like it, when I want to or need to, and even maybe mostly enjoy it." [2] How sad she has to apologize for a need that God Himself put in her—the need to be domestic.

New research indicates that the stereotype of the neurotic housewife may be just as distorted as the old picture of the happy homemaker. According to an article in *Psychology To-*

day,[3] psychologist Linda Fidell and sociologist Jan Prather interviewed three groups of housewives: (1) those who didn't work outside the home and didn't *want* to work; (2) those looking for jobs; and (3) those who had a job outside the home. They found that the happiest group of women interviewed was the first. The housewives who didn't *want* to work away from home "have happy marriages, they feel in control of their lives, and they have the best physical and mental health of the three groups."

The unhappiest group was the second, housewives seeking outside employment. These tended to have "low self-esteem, feel they are pawns of fate, and mask their loneliness and worry with drugs."[4]

For every housewife, *acceptance* is the key—acceptance of God's will for your life. In this respect, the Church in particular has failed to give young women a feeling of importance in being homemakers. We exalt the more visible achievers such as teachers, ministers, musicians and TV evangelists. We assume that these people are more important in the Church than the women who choose to stay home and raise their children. Sometimes we even try to steer mothers away from their homes.

For example, until a friend of mine had a surprise baby at age thirty-nine, she had been very active in her church leading women's Bible studies. She told me that the most difficult part of motherhood was the pressure from women in her religious community. They felt that her church service was more important than staying home, and pressed her to leave her brand new baby with sitters and continue teaching. She wisely chose to remain at home, but her story showed me how different our expectations are now than they were even twenty years ago.

I was raised in the 40s when being a wife and mother was still considered a special task. This view was reinforced by the many family orientated television shows like, *Leave It to Beaver* and *Ozzie and Harriet*. In these series, Mother was a very integral part of the family and often saved the day for Dad and kids alike.

I just assumed I would give up my career to raise a family, and as a young mother I had a support group of women behind me. They were always available to give me reassurance and help with the different and difficult phases of a homemaker's life. Many days the neighborhood mothers would congregate on someone's front steps, and while the children played together in the yard, we exchanged recipes, talked out problems and gained encouragement. Today the front steps are deserted and the young woman who chooses to stay home may find herself isolated, an oddity in a world of working women without any form of support, wondering if she has made the right decision.

A study by Myra Marx Ferree, an assistant professor of sociology at the University of Connecticut, shows that the happiest housewives are

> "women who feel that their accomplishments are recognized and who are warmly involved with social support groups. Their mothers, sisters, friends and cousins are in and out of the house all day. Their husbands value their work, and think it is an important contribution to the maintenance of the family. They are not lonely and they do not feel their efforts are wasted."[5]

In the early church the Apostle Paul instructed Titus to have the older women

> "train the younger women to love their husbands and children, to be self-controlled and pure, to be busy at home, to be kind, and to be subject to their husbands. . . .
>
> (Titus 2:4-5)

So, if the younger women are dissatisfied with their status as homemakers, it is a direct failure of us older women in the Church to train them. Since training implies leading by example rather than teaching, we first have to be satisfied with our position in life; we have to have a good self-image in the area of homemaking. Then we might consider making ourselves available to baby-sit for the young mothers, help them with housework when they are over-extended, teach them cooking and meal planning, and be there to reassure them through difficult times.

Probably one of the hardest aspects of a homemaker's life is daily housework, the continual repetitive chores that we know are going to be there tomorrow and tomorrow. Many times we find ourselves envying and resenting our husband's freedom to leave the home for work each day. I can remember days when Tom was screaming for his bottle, Shannon had just spilled her oatmeal on the floor and John, Jr. was demanding to be put on the potty at the precise moment my husband was walking out the door to go to work. I would have given anything to follow him out that door rather than face the daily chores at home. I consoled myself that at least I could take it easy on a day when I wasn't feeling up to par. My husband had to head for the office day in and day out or his family didn't eat.

Now, twenty years later, my life has changed dramatically. My husband is still going to the same job every day, but I have had an exciting collage of change and variety. At a time when my life is relatively free of household chores, my husband is more pressured than ever because of the expense of three children in college.

Maintaining a home has special responsibilities that all affect how we feel about ourselves. Plus, the job we do as homemakers affects how others think about us as well. I have observed several different kinds of homes that reflect the women who keep them. Maybe you will recognize some of them.

The Utilitarian Home

This house is well cared for, but is almost completely devoid of anything decorative or purely ornamental. Everything in it has a practical purpose. The woman who runs it is a practical-minded person, and she allows nothing "impractical" in her home or her life. Like her home, she is devoid of the feminine touches that add warmth and charm. It is hard to feel welcomed here. It is difficult to get close to this woman, for she doesn't have time to sit and talk with a friend. Everything and everybody has to have a use.

The Ultrasophisticated Home

Everything in this house has been carefully planned to have the maximum effect on visitors. Visiting this house is almost like walking through a furniture showroom: you can look, but you mustn't touch. Everything in the house, and everything in the life of the woman who lives there, is planned to impress people. She may feel shallow and does not invite close friendships because she has a fear of letting anyone see beneath the surface of her house or her life.

The Superneat Home

This home is so clean it squeaks. When you enter you realize you are on holy ground, especially when you are asked to take off your shoes. Being in this home certainly does not make one comfortable. In fact, as you visit with the lady of the house, all you can think of is your own "dirty" house and getting home to start cleaning. The lady of the house keeps jumping up rearranging a crooked picture, wiping imaginary dust from the table and even picking lint off your sweater. She believes if she controls her home she can control her life. Perhaps she is using her compulsiveness to hide from God, from others and especially from herself. Underneath the polished surface she is terribly unhappy, frightened and feeling out of control.

The Deceptive Home

On first glance, this house appears orderly and clean, for the woman of this house cleans the parts a guest will see. However, the unseen areas—the closets, dresser drawers, and laundry room—are all in a state of chaos. Inwardly, she feels that her life is like that too. The part that she exposes to the public looks like she really "has it all together"; but her soul, like her home, has dark closets and cluttered areas which she tries to hide even from God.

The Dirty Home

When you walk into this house, you need a road map to find your way through the clutter. This woman hasn't failed; she just hasn't tried. She can't cope with life, because she has allowed herself to be defeated by her self-pitying thoughts about her lot in life.

In most cases, the woman who makes no effort to keep her house in order is, consciously or subconsciously, in rebellion against her husband and ultimately against God. There is much truth in the saying that a man's home is his castle; it is also, as a rule, the fruit of his labor. Usually it has been purchased by his money, and he is working hard to keep up mortgage payments. The wife who resents her husband often punishes him by refusing to take care of the home which, more than anything else, represents his success. This woman's life is built on the principle of rebellion. She may be a very active church worker but you can be sure she is doing things *her* way, whether it is the Lord's way or not.

The Successful Home

This house is clean and orderly; yet it gives a feeling of being lived in. Special little touches in the house reflect the personality and love of the woman who cares for it. This home exudes warmth and hospitality, and the woman of the house is equally warm and hospitable. The peace you feel as you enter this house enables you to relax and to reveal the real you. You feel free to share your inner thoughts with its mistress, for she listens with interest and empathy.

Since the condition of our homes has a direct impact on our self-image, we need to find the best approach to their care. A dirty home will constantly convict us that we are worthless and lazy while a super-neat home might put us under the bondage of trying to be perfect. To find that balance is quite a task but one that can be reached by one very important biblical standard: dedication of our houses to the Lord.

I confess that I myself am a reformed "compulsive cleaner." I have already mentioned that until I became a Christian, my house had been my idol. I used it to prop up a very poor self-image, feeling somehow that having the cleanest house in the neighborhood would make me a more acceptable person. Not many people, including my family, felt comfortable in my picture-perfect home.

When I gave my house to the Lord, He had to deal with my idolatry. One of the ways He did this was to bring so many people into our home that, no matter how hard I worked, I just couldn't keep it looking perfect—especially through the three years of children's prayer meetings. Every Friday afternoon about fifty small children trooped into the house, rubbed their unwashed little hands along the walls and dirtied the carpets with their unwiped little feet. I soon realized that, although I had given my house to the Lord with my lips, I was still its owner in my heart.

I struggled with this conflict, reminding myself continually that I was only God's steward and that the ultimate responsibility for protecting the house rested in His hands. Gradually it became easier to ignore invading dirt and mud and I felt the release of knowing in my heart that my home truly *was* the Lord's house.

Actually many women who are poor housekeepers may not be so much rebellious as they are untrained. Their mothers may have failed to teach them how to organize their housework and after marriage they simply do the best they can. But then years pass and as the family grows their responsibilities and tasks reach overwhelming proportions.

These wives especially should learn to dedicate their homes to the Lord: "Commit to the Lord whatever you do, and your plans will succeed" (Proverbs 16:3). If you are cleaning your house out of obedience to Jesus, He will guide you in organizing the work.

This will help you maintain another of God's standards for proper care of your home: A good wife "watches over the affairs of her household and does not eat the bread of idleness" (Proverbs 31:27). Far too many housewives "eat the bread of idleness," sitting in front of TV screens, curling up with the latest copy of *Good Housekeeping,* or visiting with friends for hours on the telephone or over innumerable "second" cups of coffee.

"Boredom" is probably the chief complaint of the modern housewife; yet every woman's home could provide enough work to fill at least six twelve-hour days every week. The problem with these "bored" housewives is that they don't want to do, or don't know how to do, the things which need to be done so they procrastinate by "eating the bread of idleness." Then at the end of the day the sink is full of dirty dishes, the beds are unmade and the wash is still piled up in the laundry room.

Don't be intimidated by the accumulation of daily clutter: last night's newspaper scattered around the room, Jane's shoes under the kitchen table, popcorn bowls in the family room, coloring books and crayons on the dining room table, and on and on. Scripture tells us that our God is a God of order (I Corinthians 14:33), and since we are made in His image and likeness, we also function best in order. A cluttered home brings disorder to the spirit and to the mind. Plunge into the job of restoring order to your entire home. The relief of organization throughout the house will be the impetus you need to spend time cleaning special areas that need more than a fast touch of the dust rag.

Paul writes in his first letter to Timothy that young wives should "rule their household." This phrase comes from two Greek words, *oikos,* "house," and *despopes,* "master." Paul is stating another standard, that a wife has full responsibility for proper care of her home. Many women feel that the housework should be shared equally by husband and wife—and certainly when a wife is working full-time her husband should be willing to give her a hand with the household chores. Under most other circumstances, however, a husband's sphere of responsibility for the home should be confined to the yard and to certain heavy jobs that a woman isn't able to handle alone.

Since women have this responsibility, we often feel it our job to oversee even our husbands' duties. In other words, we tend to nag our husbands to do work around the house. It took me a long time to learn how negatively my husband felt about being nagged.

When a leak developed in the ceiling of our downstairs bathroom, I asked John to repair it. He got as far as removing all the loose plaster from around the leaky pipe, so that the drip would not further damage the ceiling. There he stopped.

Each week I reminded him that the pipe was still leaking and the ceiling still had a hole in it. After several months of unfruitful nagging, I remembered I had given the house to God and resigned that problem to Him, as well. Then and there, I knelt and told God that my desire was to have the bathroom repaired, but that I would let *Him* convict my husband of the need and I would not mention it again.

For *two years* the offending pipe dripped each time someone in the upstairs bathroom took a shower. Occasionally a guest would come running out of the bathroom and inform me that water was dripping from the ceiling. I refused to get upset, because by this time I knew God was trying to teach me something.

Finally, when I returned from a trip, a surprise awaited me. While I was gone, John had had the leak and ceiling repaired. At the same time, he had had carpenters finish off the basement. I had learned patience—and received a finished basement as a bonus.

God knows all about the situations He has placed us in, and He can take care of any one of them. If our desires for proper care of our homes are in accordance with His plans, it is His pleasure to fulfill them for us (see Psalm 37:4-5).

When we have met these standards, we are ready for a godly use of our homes: The Bible ordains that Christian homes are hospitable homes, for Christians are commanded to "practice hospitality ungrudgingly to one another" (I Peter 4:9).

The Bible also gives rather specific instructions regarding Christian hospitality:

First, we are to be hospitable without grumbling (I Peter 4:9). We are not to complain about the work involved, or to count the number of times we have invited Mr. and Mrs. Smith since they had us for a meal.

Second, we are to entertain not only friends and other Christians, but strangers as well:

"Do not forget to entertain strangers, for by so doing some people have entertained angels without knowing it"

(Hebrews 13:2)

Third, Jesus Himself said that we are to invite those who cannot repay us:

"When you give a luncheon or dinner, do not invite your friends, your brothers or relatives, or your rich neighbors; if you do, they may invite you back and so you will be repaid. But when you give a banquet, invite the poor, the crippled, the lame, the blind, and you will be repaid at the resurrection of the righteous"

(Luke 14:12-14)

Like most of Jesus' teachings, this one is just the opposite of the world's system which looks on entertaining as a means of advancing one's own cause, meeting the "right" people, or repaying one's social obligations.

Does it sound like housekeeping is all work and no rest? Don't worry. It isn't. The book of Ecclesiastes teaches, there is "a time for every activity under heaven"—and that includes time for resting. This is so well illustrated in the Gospel of Luke 10:38-42 when Jesus, in response to Martha's question that Mary help her, said: "Martha, Martha, you are worried and upset about many things, but only one thing is needed. Mary has chosen what is better, and it will not be taken away from her."

Mothers, especially with young children, should take advantage of their few moments of quiet during the day. This may be at nap time or while the children are outside playing. Using that time to relax, pray or meditate on a passage of Scripture will do more to make their day go smoothly than any amount of busyness. A few minutes of quiet are needed to give us a renewed perspective on our roles as the quiet, peaceful centers of family life. We are the basis of the relaxed atmosphere that every busy family needs, and if we are going to be that anchor to hold it all together, then we are going to have to be anchored to the One in whom "all things hold together" (Colossians 1:17). It is in our quiet times, when, like Mary, we sit at his feet, that we will receive the peace which we can then pass on to our husbands and children when they come home from a day of pressure. We set the atmosphere by our attitudes, and by the physical order we bring to our homes.

What a challenge to be a homemaker! We need the strength of Samson to keep our homes in good physical order, the wisdom of Solomon to rear our children, the submissiveness of Sarah to bring spiritual order, the faith of Abraham to instill faith in our family, the endurance of Job in the trials and tribulations of life, and the joy of David to keep laughter and humor abounding in the center of our home. And how wonderful that we have all we need in the Holy Spirit.

Being a homemaker is an honorable task; a full time career which will have much more far reaching effects than a weekly paycheck. It is not a time simply to endure, but a time of total commitment, directing all our energies toward the home and family. Someday, just like the housewife of Proverbs 31, there will be a season when we will reap the results of our work:

> Her children arise and call her blessed:
> her husband also, and he praises her:
> "Many women do noble things,
> but you surpass them all."
> Give her the reward she has earned.
> (Proverbs 31:28-29, 31)

It may be long in coming, but no reward will ever be more blessed.

References for Chapter 9:

1. Carol Tavris, "Women, Work Isn't Always the Answer," *Psychology Today*, (September 1976), p. 78.
2. Betty Friedan, "Why Deprive Myself of the Joys of Chicken Soup?" *Chicago Tribune*, (Thursday, April 28, 1977, Section 6), p. 1.
3. Carol Tavris, p. 78.
4. Ibid. p. 78.
5. Myra Marx Ferree, "The Confused American Housewife," *Psychology Today*, (September 1976), pp. 76, 78 & 80.

10

The Need to Be Creative

The women's liberation movement has propelled a mass exodus of mothers from the home to the working world. In the quest for self-fulfillment and further driven by divorce or economic necessity, nearly nineteen million American mothers with children under eighteen are working at full time jobs.[1] Four million mothers of children under *three* are working outside the home.[2] The dominant question of young pregnant women is no longer *when* to resign from their jobs for full-time motherhood, but rather, "How soon can I be back to work after the baby comes?" With today's modern, career oriented woman, a baby is only a minor interruption in a busy life. After six weeks of nursing a sitter is lined up and Mom is back on the job.

What effect does this have on a woman's self-image? How does the working woman, wife and mom deal with these roles? Not too well we are finding out. Studies at Texas Christian University show that many working mothers harbor strong feelings of guilt when one role suffers because of the attention required by another.[3] Women's magazines are filled with articles about anxiety and the working mother. In the course of a day, a working mother's thoughts are filled with child-related problems: *I wonder if he found his bookbag? Will she remember her key today? I hope she won't try to cook something on the stove. I'll have to tell him not to watch that scary movie on TV this afternoon.*

Some working mothers try to "make up" to their children for being away from home by excessively giving in to their wishes. The children, quick to pick up on mother's guilt, will use that as a tool to get what they want.

Some years ago, Urie Bronfenbrenner, the child-development expert, expressed alarm with the increasing trend of working mothers. In an article entitled, "Nobody Home: The Erosion of the American Family,"[4] he asked the pertinent question,

> Who is caring for America's children? Increasing numbers of children are coming home to empty houses. If there's any *reliable predictor of trouble,* it probably begins with children coming home to an empty house, whether the problem is reading difficulties, truancy, dropping out, drug addiction, or childhood depression (italics mine).

This problem is so widespread that a new term—latchkey children, since they go to school with their front-door keys strung around their necks—has been coined. One article referred to these children as a "major social problem."[5]

This is especially disheartening when mothers don't have to work to help with finances. Our neighborhood, a typical middle-class suburb, has recently experienced a wave of vandalism. According to a local junior high school principal it is almost always the work of students whose mothers have jobs away from home. These women aren't working to keep the wolf from the door; they either want to escape from their homes or to provide additional luxuries for the family.

There are women who, because of divorce or economic necessity, are forced to work. It is not a matter of affording extras, but of survival itself. For these mothers attitude is extremely important. It is not so much a question of whether she works or not, as it is how the whole family feels about her working. I believe God's protection is upon the mother who is forced by life's circumstances to work, provided she accepts her circumstances and yields her children to the Lord.

Even for these mothers though, it is not advisable to work while the child is young—the time during which bonding takes place between mother and child. One expert, Dr. Arnold Tobin, places that time between birth and sixteen months of age. He explains that during that time, there is a particular relationship between mother and child known as an "empathic tie."[6] Tobin feels that if this bond is not established, it sets a time bomb ticking during the child's infancy which will go off in adolescence. He feels that many of the distressing number of teen suicides result from the lack of this bonding. If the mother returns to work too early the tie may not be formed.

Dr. Tobin, who has seen the results in children who were denied the bonding process, has reached this conclusion:

> I have strong feelings that a woman who has a baby has agreed to a full-time job. If a woman just wants a toy, she is going to pay a price. Women are responsible for looking into themselves to ask why they want a child and to determine what kinds of gratifications they expect.[7]

The problem of bonding is further threatened by either the absence or multiplicity of caretakers. A growing child needs a stable relationship; someone who is there to understand, protect and reassure, someone who gets excited about his accomplishments and is intensely involved with every aspect of his life. If that person is missing, the child will lack a sense of being precious, valuable to his parents which may result in emotional emptiness or depression later in his life.

And rather than drawing the father and children together, a mother's working can even lessen a father's standing with the children. A 1982 study conducted by the National Institute of Mental Health reported a tendency for sons from unskilled and semi-skilled working groups who had full-time working mothers to be less admiring of their fathers.[8] It's easy to see how a child may feel his father has failed as a provider.

Like all mothers, I sometimes thought my children were so involved with their friends and their activities that they didn't even notice my existence. But when they stepped inside the door each day after school, their first word was "Mom?" Usually they didn't want anything except assurance that I was there—security.

With all these factors at work it is no wonder a working mother's self-image can suffer. When young women who feel unfulfilled in their homes seek a boost from outside employment, they usually find themselves suffering more than ever from the negative consequences of a poor self-image. Nothing is as destructive to the self-image as being a working wife who is torn by the guilt and anxiety of how her job is affecting her family. Since she feels she can't do both effectively, she does the best she can—which is never enough. Always trying to make up to someone—her boss, her children, her husband, she is a prime target for physical disorders.

Dr. Selye feels that the more the "women's movement permits women to take what have usually been considered male jobs, the more women are subject to so-called male diseases—often related to stress—such as cardiac infarctions, gastric ulcers and hypertension."[9] One professor at Cambridge even found that over-working produces hormone changes in women: Some have to shave everyday like men, while others begin to go bald or develop hairy chests. He said it is vital that women recognize their limits before it is too late.

We need to realize that giving birth and raising children is a built-in, God-given desire. In Old Testament times it was considered deplorable if a woman was barren. Perhaps childlessness meant being deprived of the privilege of participating in God's very own work, that of building people to establish His kingdom. Hannah prayed with such emotion for a child that the priest of the temple chided her, thinking she was drunk (I Samuel 1:9-18). We can imagine that Sarah must have prayed for a child all her life until she got too old for childbearing and gave up. Probably it was the same with Elizabeth, John the Baptist's mother.

We women today are not all that different from our ancestors once we get beneath the veneer put on to convince a world whose values have changed. For a woman to have a child still means the fulfillment of her deepest creative urge.

So why is it that some women look upon caring for their own children as too boring and tedious to be worthy of their full time and effort? Possibly because they don't bring to it the sense of excitement and urgency we bring to undertakings we *see* as creative. Someone who sets out to paint a large landscape will choose his oils, canvas and easel with care, plan the foreground, the background, what elements to accentuate, where to make delicate brush strokes and where to highlight, and then proceed according to his plan with intensity and purpose until the work is finished. So will one who is writing a book or building a bridge or establishing a business. If any of these ventures was done haphazardly with the apathetic attitude some people have toward raising children, no one would be surprised if the outcome were fairly dismal. We need to dedicate ourselves to our youngsters until they get older. Then it could be time to consider new avenues.

Perhaps a mother of grown children could go back to school

and prepare for a career or just take a part-time job to supplement her husband's income since expenses are usually greater with older children.

For a woman who has kept house twenty years and reared children to adulthood, it really may be time to expand her horizons. So many women experience the "empty nest syndrome" after their children are grown that a job later in life has a positive effect. In fact, we should prepare while the children are young for the time when we will have more freedom. The Proverbs 31 woman had a job at some period in her life also. The Amplified Bible makes plain that it was at a time when she had more freedom.

> She considers a new field before she buys or accepts it—expanding prudently (and *not courting neglect of her present duties by assuming others*) With her savings (of time and strength) she plants fruitful vines in her vineyard (italics added).

The Book of Ecclesiastes tells us that there is a time for everything (Ecclesiastes 3:1), even a job.

My friend Carol illustrated this point. She was a working wife and mother when she and her husband Bob joined our Fellowship eight years ago. She had taken a job when her little boy was just three years old, in order to pay off some large medical bills. Bob's semi-invalid mother lived with them and took care of little Jon while Carol worked.

Long after the medical bills were paid, Carol continued to work so that they could afford the "extras" Bob's salary did not permit. She had credit cards for many of the better stores in Chicago and spent money freely. Each time she bought some luxury item, she told herself, "I deserve this because I'm working so hard," but she and Bob both felt guilt and pressure from the arrangement.

After becoming a Christian, Carol began to feel she should stay at home. When Bob concurred, Carol resigned her job and Bob took over the finances. The next six months were difficult, as Carol struggled with her feelings of rebellion and resentment about not having any money of her own to spend, but they have been rewarded: Carol and Bob now have a savings account, something they never had in all the years when they were bringing in two salaries. Carol's Christmas present to Bob that year was all her charge cards wrapped up in a gift package.

Carol says that God gave her a gift of stretching their money so that they never lacked for anything. She became an inventive and creative homemaker, searching out bargains in food, furniture and clothing. She and Bob are hospitable Christians and entertain frequently—all on one salary.

Carol's self-image improved after she quit work; she knew that she was in the place God had assigned to her. She was never bored. God gave her a ministry of counseling other women in addition to her gift of running her household economically.

After eight years of being a homemaker, Carol's situation has again changed. Her mother-in-law's death and her son Jon's departure for college, left Carol with a lot of time on her hands. Also, her husband's salary was no longer adequate to cover college expenses, so Carol began searching for a job. She was often reminded that her office skills were no longer current, but Carol was sure God was leading her to get back into the working world, so she began to pray that *He* would find her a job. Several days later a cousin called to say her neighbor was looking for an assistant in his office. Carol applied for the job and was hired without even filling out an application.

She has had to learn many new skills but with the assurance that God has given her the job, she feels confident to tackle them.

Carol's self-image has had a tremendous boost. At an age when many women feel their main purpose in life has been achieved and they are not making a worthwhile contribution, Carol knows that her financial assistance is easing the burden on her husband for their son's education. There was a time for Carol to give up her desire to work. Now God, in His time, has given her a new job and a new sense of self-worth. It's all in the timing.

Until the time comes to pursue a job outside the home, however, there are many creative outlets for busy homemakers.

One special outlet for a woman's innate creativity is in her relationships—with her husband, her family and her neighbors. Relationships don't just happen. If they thrive and grow and mature, it is because someone spends time and energy fostering them. Each one of our children is a special and unique individual. Rather than treating them all the same, we mothers have the challenge of discovering each one's potential and hidden resources. This takes large blocks of time, and more energy, insight and innovative ideas than any of us has at the outset. Now that my children are older, I can see that I have a different relationship with each one of them. It didn't happen overnight, but developed slowly over the years as I took the time to learn about their dreams, desires and goals, and also to share personal aspects of my life with them. As they grew up, we added a new dimension to our relationship—that of friend.

Within a marriage, too, we can ignore everything about a spouse except surface traits, his obvious talents and even more obvious failures, until soon there is nothing except the dry husks of duty to keep the marriage standing. If, on the other hand, it is to be a marriage of excitement and mutual growth and joy, we must maintain an alertness to inner feeling and need.

God has given women the intuitiveness to be especially proficient in human relationships. To develop the most potential in our husbands and children is a challenge demanding the maximum of our creative talents. From our homes, such sensitivity will spill over to others—a sister having marital difficulties, the lonely widow down the block, a young person living in confusion.

Now you may feel that you have no talent or creative ability. I firmly believe that God, our Creator, has instilled some of His creativity into each of His children, and if we fail to find an outlet for the "bonus" He has given us we will be frustrated. Since we are made in the image of God we, too, must have the satisfaction of seeing the work of our hands and saying, "It is good."

If you really don't know what your special abilities might be, I suggest that you ask your husband. Many times he will have a God-given recognition of talents of which you are not aware. I was very surprised at what my husband suggested for me.

One night as we were getting ready for bed, he offered, "You know, I think you should write a book." The idea was so preposterous that I started to laugh.

"You must be crazy," I replied, "you know I hate to write."

As I settled down to go to sleep, I kept thinking about his remark. *After living with me for fifteen years, he should know I don't have any literary ability. Doesn't he have to prod me even to write a simple thank-you note? Well, he certainly was wrong there.*

Yet the very next day, I felt an odd, unexpected excitement about the prospect of writing, and decided to tackle it. It took a lot of work, some struggling through discouragement but the thrill of seeing my first book published outweighed any frustration. My husband had this insight before I did, so if your husband suggests that you learn to sew, take an accounting course, or study the piano, allow him—and yourself—the dignity of considering it. *Pay attention.* God may be speaking through him.

My sister, Jeannie, used to say that she was the only person God forgot to instill with a bit of creativity. She said that anyone who still drew stick people at the age of forty couldn't be very artistic. Because of that, I was quite surprised when I dropped by her home one day and she proudly displayed a needlepoint picture she had just finished. Now she is collecting antiques and cleaning and restoring them for her home.

When Susan and Bob bought a used piano for their children, Susan decided to fulfill her long-cherished dream of learning to play. At thirty-seven she knew she would not become a concert pianist, but there was an unfulfilled need in her which she wanted to express. Now she plays for her own enjoyment, and one of the side effects of piano lessons has been an increase in discipline in other areas of her life.

Women with poor self-images usually have not developed their creative skills. They do not see themselves as clever or talented people and they live up to their negative view. Attempting something artistic can have a tremendously positive effect on self-image and also on femininity. Creating beautiful needlepoint, a watercolor or centerpiece seems to enhance the deepest meaning of being feminine. It is important that we define ourselves in ways other than wife and mother.

Early in our marriage, I found a hobby that not only fulfilled my need to be creative but also increased my sense of personal worth by helping furnish our home. Since my husband and I were married while he was still in school, most of our furnishings were someone else's hand-me-downs. When I learned to refinish furniture, I could turn Aunt Mary's old dining room table into a gorgeous piece of furniture—finished to my own taste and showing the results of my hard work. When John proudly pointed out my handiwork to our visitors my self-image soared. I can honestly say I never envied the new furniture some of our friends could afford because the pieces I had refinished seemed so special. And a large part of the fun was browsing through used furniture stores for bargains.

The "good wife" described in Proverbs 31 had a hobby which she also turned into a profitable business venture. "She selects wool and flax and works with eager hands. . . . In her hand she holds the distaff and grasps the spindle with her fingers" (verses 13 and 19).

When we feel like sewing we have only to choose from bolts of beautiful material displayed in air-conditioned stores. The woman in Proverbs first had to make the thread and weave it into cloth before she could clothe her household in scarlet (verse 21), making clothing of "fine linen and purple" for herself; (verse 22) and then making linen garments and girdles for sale (verse 24). No wonder, as it says in verse 27, she did not "eat the bread of idleness"!

After the Proverbs wife had taken care of her family's needs and her own, she used her creative ability to make a little spending money on the side. God's blessing was upon her business venture, for verse 18 says, "She perceives that her merchandise is profitable."

It may be that some hobby begun as an outlet for your creativity while your children are young may develop into a profitable business when they are older and no longer require most of your time. A supplemental source of income during the years your children are in college would certainly be welcome in most families.

In today's culture, most young ladies are no longer taught the fine arts of needlework, or even the basic skills of sewing and cooking. Instead, they are prepared for careers and urged to compete with men for "equal job opportunities." But the appearance of large hobby stores in many of the suburban shopping malls indicates that women—and men too—are recognizing the need to be creative. There has been a tremendous resurgence of interest in such long forgotten skills as quilting and weaving. Perhaps it is the result of a subconscious desire to return to an earlier time when life was less complicated and women had a clearly defined role in society. The desire to be creative is a divinely placed need and, even when our children are small and we never seem to have enough hours in the day, we need some form of creative recreation.

Three things happen when you make the time to work on a special project: First, it gives you relaxation and a welcome change from the tedium of daily chores; second, it gives you an incentive to do your housework more efficiently and quickly; third, it enhances your self-image and reassures you of your individuality. When you are "expressing yourself" in creating an object of beauty and usefulness, a culinary work of art, or a musical or literary masterpiece, you are no longer just John's wife or Tommy's mother; you are an individual with a God-given talent which can be used to produce a work of art that bears the stamp of your own unique personality. Also, a creative endeavor is one of the few things in life we can do without comparing or competing with others. We do it because we choose to and if we like it—that is enough.

There is another benefit of creative endeavors that needs to be mentioned. Although a young family requires a tremendous commitment of our time and energy, we need to be careful that we don't make the care and feeding of our children our entire lives. From the time a child begins kindergarten, he starts that long process of separating himself from his mother. The mother who has nothing else in her life will find it hard to let go. If, however, she has developed other areas, she will use her free time as an opportunity to continue her development in creative pursuits, Christian service and perhaps, even a new career.

Our self-image will be enhanced and strengthened when we recognize, embrace and act upon the special creative flow God has placed deeply in the center of our being. Whether our creativity is directed toward relationships with our children, husbands or neighbors, a job or a work of art, we will be more complete and fulfilled persons as we allow God to develop the special gifts and talents He has deposited within us.

References for Chapter 10:

1. Marion Long, "Do Working Women Make Good Moms?" *Chicago Sun Times,* Family Weekly, (May 8, 1983), pp. 4-5.

2. Maryann B. Brinley with Sanford Matthews, M.D., "How to Have A Baby, Work Full Time and Hold Back the Tears," *McCall's,* (July 1983), pp. 30, 34, 36, 38, 40, 116, 118 & 120.

3. John E. Gibson, "Guilt! Can You Recognize it Without Feeling It?" *Chicago Sun Times,* Family Weekly, (June 7, 1981), p. 25.

4. Urie Bronfenbrenner, "Nobody Home: The Erosion of the American Family," *Psychology Today,* V. 10, (May 1977), pp. 41 & 45.

5. B. Brooker, "The LatchKey Problem: Children Who Go Home to An Empty House," *Chicago Daily News,* (January 29, 1977), Everyweek, pp. 1 & 20.

6. April Olzak, "Teen Suicide and the North Shore Connection," *Chicago Tribune Magazine,* (July 27, 1980), pp. 13-21.

7. Ibid.

8. Long, pp. 4-5.

9. Hans Selye, "To Beat Stress—Learn How to Live," *Reader's Digest,* (July 1977), pp. 161-163.

11

Accepting Your Roles

> Husbands . . . be considerate as you live with your wives, and treat them with respect as the *weaker* partner and as heirs with you of the gracious gift of life, so that nothing will hinder your prayers.
>
> (I Peter 3:7, italics added)

This is a scripture that causes feminists to grind their teeth and rant that the Bible is a sexist book. I don't believe that Peter, who was a married man (Mark 1:30), had any idea how much reaction he would cause by the inclusion of this one verse in his letter. Although women are the weaker sex by distribution of body musculature and bone structure, we miss Peter's point if we don't see beyond the physical differences. I believe Peter was also speaking of the wife as the more sensitive sex, which is backed up biologically and psychologically. Therefore, he cautions husbands to "be considerate," "live understandingly" (ML), "be . . . thoughtful of their needs" (LB). Peter knows how fragile a woman's self-esteem is and how easily her conscience can be violated. Certainly, a woman's self-image is set at a much more delicate balance than a man's. Men do have their weak spots but, generally they deal with the normal wear and tear of life in a manner which makes us women wonder if they might be a little thick. I used to remark jokingly that my husband was almost impossible to insult. He didn't seem to take offense at remarks that would have sent me to the bedroom in tears.

God, who designed us as the more delicate, sensitive model of *homo sapiens,* also knew we needed greater protection than the durable male model. He has provided that protection through our fathers, pastors and husbands. This is why Paul says that "the head of the woman is man" (I Corinthians 11:3). A little later in that same chapter, Paul adds that this is why women wear a covering on their heads. It is a sign of their spiritual covering, of being under authority (verse 10).

We see a beautiful example of this covering in the book of Ruth. Ruth goes to harvest in the field of her kinsman, Boaz. After taking notice of her, Boaz instructs Ruth to remain in his field and says, "I have told the young men not to touch you" (Ruth 2:9). Boaz provided the physical protection she needed, for she might otherwise be taken advantage of. She was a foreigner and a young widow without a livelihood with no one to avenge her if she was wronged.

Naomi, Ruth's mother-in-law, decided that Ruth should go to Boaz while he was sleeping on the threshing floor. Since the nearest kinsman had the right to marry a widow, Ruth could let him know she would be pleased to be his wife even though she had a closer kinsman. So Ruth went down to the threshing floor and, following her mother-in-law's advice, lay down at Boaz' feet. Sometime later, Boaz awakened and was startled to see Ruth. She said, "spread the corner of your garment over me, since you are a kinsman-redeemer" (Ruth 3:9). This was a custom from patriarchal times, when marriage and kinship went hand in hand. The spreading of the covering symbolized the marriage covenant.

The spiritual force of this message is demonstrated in Ezekiel 16:8:

> Later I passed by, and when I looked at you and saw
> that you were old enough for love, I spread the corner
> of my garment over you and covered your nakedness.
> I gave you my solemn oath and entered into a cove-
> nant with you, declares the Sovereign Lord, and you
> became mine.

God, through the sacrifice of His Son, Jesus, has "covered"
our sin and nakedness. Although Jesus is our covering before
God, the man is God's earthly representative of that covering: "A
man ought not to cover his head, since he is the image and glory
of God; but the woman is the glory of man. For man did not
come from woman, but woman from man; neither was man
created for woman, but woman for man" (I Corinthians 11:7-8).

God has created us women to be under a man's authority. I do
not mean we are to allow ourselves to be abused either physically or verbally, but our position Biblically is clear: "The head
of the woman is man," and rebelling against it will only hurt us.

Romans 13:2-5, for instance, seems to indicate that there is a
definite correlation between rebellion and fear. Paul ends his
discussion on authority with the statement: "Therefore, it is
necessary to submit to the authorities, not only because of
possible punishment but also because of *conscience*" (verse 5).
Since we women have the more delicate and sensitive conscience, rebellion (manifested by lack of submission to authority) will cause us many negative emotions, especially fear. This
may be why women have so many more problems with fears
and phobias than men.

I was a very rebellious young woman and wife. Since I also
had a very negative self-image, I suffered numerous fears. After I
became a Christian and learned about the protection God
provided through my husband, I began to move under that
covering. One of the first things I noticed was that my fears
began to disappear. No longer did I lie in bed nights quaking at

every noise when my husband was away. I would get into bed, say a short prayer and fall soundly asleep. My fear of airplanes was even worse than my fear of being alone. Waves of fear and anxiety would wash over me for weeks before I went on a trip. The whole time I was flying I would sit frozen, gripping the seat with a death-like vise. That fear, too, disappeared completely.

I found it extremely healing to my self-image to be free from so many of the fears that had crippled my life. Fear not only prevents us from doing many of the things we would like to do but it makes us despise ourselves for being dominated by emotions. When I was able to get on an airplane without sweaty palms and a nervous stomach, stay alone in the house without my husband, and meet a new group of people without feeling like I had nothing to say, my self-image increased immeasurably.

If God in His goodness and concern for our delicate internal mechanism has provided covering and protection for us, why are we so reluctant to accept His gift? Why do we picket for our rights, demand that "him" be changed to "person" and declare Paul a chauvinist? Not only do we fight against God's provision, but we cause ourselves mental and physical problems by our lack of covering and protection.

Over the years I have seen sincere Christian women, many in ministry, get into various forms of deception. I often wondered why women seem more susceptible than men to religious discord, and why spiritual matters appear to have greater appeal for the female sex. For the answers to these questions, I began (where else?) at the beginning.

> So the Lord caused the man to fall into a deep sleep; and while he was sleeping, he took one of the man's ribs and closed up the place with flesh. Then the Lord God made a woman from the rib he had taken out of the man, and he brought her to the man.
> The man said, "This is now bone of my bones and

> flesh of my flesh; she shall be called 'woman,' for she
> was taken out of man."
>
> (Genesis 2:21-23)

Why didn't God form Eve out of the dust of the ground, as He had formed Adam? Why did He create her from a part of the man? I believe God wanted woman to know from the very beginning that she is *dependent* on man. I also believe Eve resented her dependent position, and this resentment made her susceptible to Satan's temptation:

> "You will not surely die," the serpent said to the
> woman. "For God knows that when you eat of it
> your eyes will be opened, and you will be like
> God, knowing good and evil"
>
> (Genesis 3:4-5)

According to Watchman Nee, "the meaning of the tree of the knowledge of good and evil is *independence,* the taking of independent action. The tree of life, though, signifies *dependence* or reliance on God."[1]

Why did Satan approach Eve rather than Adam with the temptation to take independent action? Was it because he recognized Eve's resentment against God for making her dependent? We know that we can only be tempted when there is something within us that gives "the tempter" a beachhead: "but each one is tempted when, *by his own evil desire,* he is dragged away and enticed (James 1:14, italics added). Eve certainly was dragged away from Adam's side—symbolic of his covering and protection—and lured into the sin that brought death for all mankind.

Satan knew that Eve was ripe for the temptation to be independent from God and to discover spiritual truths ahead of Adam. Perhaps Eve thought that if she could become "like God," she could make Adam spiritually dependent on her as she had been dependent on him for her creation. Women have not changed a great deal through the ages.

I have noticed in our Fellowship that, as with most Christian couples, it is usually the wife who accepts Christ first. If she then comes under her husband's authority, he is likely to become a strong, dynamic Christian. If she will not relinquish her position as leader in the family, her husband most often remains a weak and ineffectual Christian if, indeed, he becomes a Christian at all.

We women are undoubtedly the daughters of our mother Eve, who brought sin into the world by stepping out from under her husband's authority into independence. Therefore, when God restores a marriage, it is usually *after* the wife has renounced her inheritance from the sin of Eve by stepping back into a position of dependence upon her husband. We wives must restore to our husbands the decision-making authority before God will give them *spiritual* authority.

A fault among Christian women is to think that we are more "spiritual" than our husbands. It is probably true that we do find it easier to accept the supernatural aspects of the Christian faith and that we spend more time in religious (not necessarily spiritual) activities. What we often lack, however, is discernment. Let's face it: Since the beginning, our sex has been more easily deceived. "For Adam was formed first, then Eve. And Adam was not the one deceived; it was the *woman who was deceived* and became a sinner" (I Timothy 2:13-14, italics added).

Many enlightened Christians believe we are entering the time that Jesus spoke about on the Mount of Olives:

> For false Christs and false prophets will appear and perform great signs and miracles to deceive even the elect—if that were possible.
>
> (Matthew 24:24)

In these last days, according to Paul, men will

> worm their way into homes and gain control over
> weak-willed women, who are loaded down with sins
> and are swayed by all kinds of evil desires, always
> learning but never able to acknowledge the truth.
>
> (II Timothy 3:6-7)

The women Paul had in mind are those who eagerly learn and listen to anyone preaching some new experience—those who grab indiscriminately all that is offered in the name of Jesus Christ without ever testing the spirit behind the offering.

When your husband, father or pastor reacts adversely to the "spiritual insights" and experiences that you try to share with him, pay attention. It may be that he is discerning deception. Men seem to have a natural ability to cut through religious trappings and discern spiritual truth or error. So if your husband is just a natural kind of guy and not what you would call "religious," praise God. He's just what you need.

Women seem to be naturally drawn to Bible studies and prayer meetings. We enjoy listening to testimonies and reading spiritual books. But we must be careful not to engage in activities that make us *feel* spiritual but do not demand an inner change. It is a humbling thing (I speak from experience) for the Christian wife to realize that, in spite of all her religious activities, her husband's life may be a much better witness than hers.

Any woman who seeks a ministry—a God-directed service such as teaching—is especially vulnerable to the temptation of Eve. She is usually a gifted person, and is deceived into thinking that if she submits to her husband she will not be able to use her gifts. The tempter *wants* her to pervert them. If God has given you a gift—whether a natural talent or a supernatural gift of the Spirit—He certainly wants you to use it. *But only under authority!* A person who employs the gifts of the Holy Spirit without submitting to guidance and authority is like a teenager who takes the family car for a "joy ride" before he has learned to drive. What is intended to be a great boon becomes, in unskilled and undirected hands, an instrument of destruction—both for the user and for others.

Is a woman *allowed* to have a ministry? God has given legitimate ministries to many women, but there are two very practical guidelines that must be observed. One is found in these words of Jesus:

> He who is faithful in a very little is faithful also in much; and he who is dishonest in a very little is dishonest also in much.
>
> (Luke 16:10, RSV)

This principle of faithfulness has a broad application. We must be responsible for the things God has put in our lives, such as care of our bodies or housework, as well as our relationship with the man God has put in authority over us, in order to be entrusted with a ministry.

A second guideline is found in Paul's first letter to the Corinthians: "The spiritual did not come first, but the natural, and after that the spiritual" (I Corinthians 15:46). Every woman, whether single or married, has certain responsibilities in the natural, or physical, realm, which must be met before she can assume responsibilities in the spiritual realm. And not one of these natural areas should be allowed to suffer as the result of her ministry. In other words, if you are able to take care of all your natural responsibilities and still have a ministry, then you are in God's will. *But to the extent that any of these natural areas suffer, to that extent you are out of the will of God.*

This was the case with a woman who came to me once for counseling because of her poor relationship with her husband. She was extremely active in church work, but I told her that none of her religious activities was in the will of God. She was completely taken aback until I explained that God had given her natural responsibilities—home, husband, children—which were being neglected and that He would not entrust the "true riches" of a spiritual ministry to her until she reset her priorities.

No matter how gifted a woman may be, God will never violate one of His principles. We either do it God's way or He lets us fail in our way.

Moses' sister, Miriam, had a wonderful ministry. She is the first prophetess mentioned in the Bible and, with Moses and Aaron, was one of the leaders of Israel. As long as she remained under Moses' authority, God blessed her ministry. But her desire for independence and human recognition finally led to her downfall. In the book of Numbers we read:

> Miriam and Aaron began to talk against Moses because of his Cushite wife, for he had married a Cushite. "Has the Lord spoken only through Moses?" they asked. "Hasn't he also spoken through us?". . .
> The anger of the Lord burned against them, and he left them. When the cloud lifted from above the Tent, there stood Miriam—leprous, like snow.
> (Numbers 12: 1-2,9-10)

Why was Miriam alone punished, when both she and Aaron had spoken against Moses? My guess is that Miriam initiated this action and persuaded her brother Aaron to join her—just as Eve talked Adam into sharing with her the forbidden fruit. Miriam, like Eve, resented being in a secondary and dependent position. She longed for the human recognition that is accorded to the person in authority.

The same temptation comes to every woman in a ministry. Sooner or later, she may hear a whisper in her ear, "You are so much more spiritual than your husband! Why does he always get to make the final decision?" Or, "If you submit to him completely you will never get to have any ministry at all."

If a woman is wise, she will run to the cover of her husband's authority the minute she becomes aware of this temptation. Unfortunately, many women become convinced that they are indeed much more capable than their husbands and really *should* be in a position of leadership. The longer they contunue in that direction, the harder it will be to change course. This temptation must be recognized at the start for what it is: a lie to destroy her and her ministry.

Some women take part in numerous spiritual activities but have difficulty really helping others. They are always seeking more counsel, another book, or the right word to set them free. In Isaiah 58 God promises that if we will minister to the needs of others—sharing our food with the hungry, providing a home for the homeless, clothing the naked—then our "healing will quickly appear" (verse 8). Not only that, but God promises to guide us, strengthen us and satisfy our needs (verse 11). It is important that we give out to others what God has given to us. In this way we will be continually emptying ourselves for God to fill us again. Also, the surest way to improve our self-image is to allow God to let us be His instrument of blessing in another's life.

On the other hand, some women are constantly giving of themselves in service to others, but never take time to receive from God. Since they do not spend time alone with Him, their good works are done by human strength and cannot minister to the spiritual needs of others.

The balance between giving and receiving is most important. We cannot give to others what we have not first received from God, and we must give after we have received. There should be a continuous flow of life from God to us, and from us to others. In this way, both we and our ministries will be kept fresh and vital.

What are legitimate ministries for women, according to the

Word of God? The "good wife" of Proverbs 31 had two: a ministry of giving, or good works, "She opens her arms to the poor, and extends her hands to the needy" (verse 20) and a ministry of teaching, "She opens her mouth with skillful and godly Wisdom, and in her tongue is the law of kindness—giving counsel and instruction" (verse 26, Amplified).

First, she was somehow involved in ministering to the poor and needy. "She opens her arms" indicates a generous giving of material possessions. Those of us who belong to the great American middle class sometimes forget that, even in this land of plenty, people go to bed hungry. It is unfortunate that the terms "good works" and "do-gooder" are spoken with scorn in so many churches today. Even though we are saved by faith, not by works (Ephesians 2:8-9), we must never overlook the balancing scriptures found in Ephesians 2:10, in Titus 2:14, and in James 2:18. Nor do we dare lose sight of Jesus' parable of the sheep and the goats (Matthew 25:31-46). It is frightening to read the fate of those who failed to give food and drink and clothing to those who had need of them, to show hospitality to strangers, and to visit hospitals and prisons.

If our faith in Jesus Christ does not produce good works, there are many who will never want to share that faith. In many cases a person's physical needs are so great that he isn't even aware of his spiritual needs. Unless we demonstrate *our* love to a starving man by supplying him with food, he will not listen when we talk to him about *God's* love. Here again, "the spiritual did not come first, but the natural, and after that the spiritual."

Women, it seems, are particularly adapted to the "good works" ministries. In the early church, widows over sixty years of age qualified for assistance only if they had "practiced hospitality . . . washed the feet of the saints . . . relieved the afflicted, and . . . been devoted to all kinds of good works" (I Timothy 5:10, ML). Paul exhorts Christian women to adorn themselves with good works rather than costly apparel (I Timothy 2:9-10).

One version says that "Christian women should be noticed for being kind and good" (LB).

The Bible contains many examples of generous women who, like the Proverbs wife, opened their hands to the poor and reached out to the needy. Among them are: the widow who shared with Elijah her last bit of oil and meal (I Kings 17:10-15); Peter's mother and Martha, both of whom had the privilege of showing hospitality to our Lord Himself; and Dorcas, one of the very few people whose resurrection from the dead is recorded in the Bible.

Hers is a good example of service. Dorcas fell sick and the disciples sent for Peter, but, by the time he arrived, she was already dead and "all the widows stood around him crying and showing him the robes and other clothing that Dorcas had made while she was still with them" (Acts 9:39). I can just picture poor Peter standing among all those weeping and wailing women. No wonder he put them all out of the room. When he prayed, God raised her from the dead and "this became known all over Joppa, and many people believed in the Lord" (verse 42).

Dorcas was a woman who probably did not consider herself very gifted. There is no record of her prophesying or evangelizing or teaching, as other women did in those days (see Acts 21:9; John 4:39; and Acts 18:26); but she *could* sew, and she employed that ability to the fullest (Acts 9:39). God richly rewarded this ministry of good works by bringing her back to life and then using her death and resurrection as the vehicle through which many were brought to belief in Jesus Christ (Acts 9:42).

The good wife not only opened her arms to the poor; she also extended her hands to "the needy" whether in body, mind or spirit (Proverbs 31:26, Amplified). As this translation indicates, "the needy" includes people with spiritual and emotional as well as physical needs.

There are many ways in which a woman can minister to the

needs of those around her: baking a cake for a neighbor, babysitting for a young mother, visiting an elderly person in a retirement home, listening to a friend share her heartache, remembering to send that birthday card, or baking cookies for the Christmas party in your child's classroom. These aren't "spiritual" activities and they don't lead to public recognition. But if they are done from the pure motive of love, they are pleasing to God and will eventually bring glory to His name.

Ministries of healing, evangelism, teaching, and prophecy are exciting, but they carry with them a danger that the glory might be given to the healer, evangelist, teacher or prophet rather than to God. But good works and acts of mercy are not done in the public eye, and if we follow the biblical injunction not to let our left hand know what the right is doing (Matthew 6:3), the glory will go to God, not to us.

In addition to her ministry of good works, the Proverbs 31 lady had a teaching ministry. One aspect of a woman's teaching ministry is clarified in Paul's letter to Titus:

> The older women . . . are to teach what is good, and so train the young women to love their husbands and children, to be sensible, chaste, domestic, kind, and submissive to their husbands, that the word of God may not be discredited.
>
> (Titus 2:3-5, RSV)

Women are not only to teach other women, but also to train them. In other words, disciple them and guide them by their example. This teaching and training is directed at a practical goal: that of being good wives and mothers. We are to teach all things that will lead to a development of the fullest potential of women.

If you are being taught the Word of God in a Bible-study group but are not seeing any changes in your life, you are merely acquiring knowledge. Find a group where you not only will be taught what the Word of God says, but will be trained in applying God's Word to your daily life. Then you will begin to see your life come into harmony.

Church leaders are recognizing God's anointing on gifted women; we are no longer limited to teaching only women and children. We should be aware, however, of the caution expressed to those who would desire to teach Scripture: "Not many of you should presume to be teachers, my brothers [or sisters], because you know that we who teach will be judged more strictly" (James 3:1).

I have seen many women rush into the ministry of teaching who were later "judged" by their own words. We have to understand clearly that if we are teaching what we are not living God will expose the lie. We better be sure it is God who has called us into teaching and not our desire to be recognized. One sure way of knowing we have God's approval is to know we have the approval of the authority in our lives. If we do, we can have the assurance that any judgment God brings in our lives is for our benefit and the good of those we are instructing and will not harm us.

Women can have great freedom in the church today. We are allowed to lead worship, prophesy, speak in tongues, teach, pray for healing and employ all the gifts of the Holy Spirit. Actually, a woman's sensitive spirit makes her an ideal vessel of the Holy Spirit in the administration of His gifts, as long as we do not usurp the authority of the men placed over us as a covering (I Timothy 2:11-12). True, the governmental aspects of church life are conferred upon the men, but I see this as God's recognition of our special gifts and limitations. I enjoy the freedom I have as a woman; I can minister and use the gifts God has given me, but I am also free from the worries and problems of leadership.

In order to prepare for any ministry, I have found that a daily quiet time with the Lord is my most important "spiritual activity." God can fill and refresh us best when we take time to meditate on His Word and allow Him to speak to us and minster to our needs. Peter knew this when he stated: "Do you want more and more of God's kindness and peace? Then learn to know him better and better" (II Peter 1:2, LB). It is by learning to know God that we will deepen our relationship with Him. As we learn who He is and how He loves us, our self-esteem will increase significantly.

As a mother of four children, I know how hard it is to have a daily quiet time. Once I tried to set aside a regular period of time for meditation and prayer, but I found myself in bondage to my fixed schedule. I learned to be flexible and take whatever time the Lord provided. Sometimes it was in the morning, sometimes at night just before bedtime. It was as long as an hour or as short as five minutes; it might have been in my living room or in the car driving to the store—but always the Lord provided *some* time for me to be alone with Him.

Sometimes the time was there but I avoided it. I was usually not conscious of doing that until I would realize that I had substituted legitimate pursuits for my quiet time. The activities were necessary, but they were keeping me from something more important.

At other times I found I was covering over some matter that I didn't want to deal with: unforgiveness, lack of obedience, reluctance to release a situation to the Lord, any one of a number of things. I know now that if I do not take the time for prayer, I will soon be clogged up with sin and my spiritual life will be almost non-existent. Oh, I may continue with spiritual activities, but I am no longer "abiding in the vine" (John 15:1-8). If however, I seek His cleansing daily, I will continue to be in the presence of God. Therefore, I can turn any moment such as waiting in a long grocery line into a time of fellowship with Him.

I need that for my own ministry of caring for my family, for I am indispensable only to my husband and children. Women will read many books and hear other teachers, but my children will have only one mother and (I hope!) my husband will have only one wife. Secure under my husband's authority, my ministry is to "love my husband and children, to be sensible, chaste, domestic, kind, and submissive to my husband, that the Word of God may not be discredited."

Reference for Chapter 11:

1. Watchman Nee, *The Latent Power of the Soul,* Christian Fellowship Publishers, Inc., (New York, N.Y., 1972), p. 38.

12

Achieving the Delicate Balance

One day a lawyer came to Jesus and asked him, "Sir, which is the most important command in the laws of Moses?" Jesus replied:

> "Love the Lord your God with all your heart, soul, and mind." This is the first and greatest commandment. The second most important is similar, "Love your neighbor *as much as you love yourself.*"
>
> (Matthew 22:36-39, LB; italics added)

As much as I love myself? If that's the case, our neighbors are in for very scarce rations. For most of us, it's not a question of loving ourselves, often we don't even *like* who we are.

Wander through any Christian bookstore. You will find many books on self-esteem, positive thinking or dealing with issues such as anger and guilt that keep us from loving ourselves. It seems so simple. Why can't we just believe the Word of God when He tells us, "I have loved you with an everlasting love; I have drawn you with loving-kindness" (Jeremiah 31:3). Scripture is full of references of God's love for us. Furthermore, God not only tells us how precious we are to Him, He demonstrated

His love by sending His only Son to suffer and die for us. "This is how we know what love is: Jesus Christ laid down his life for us" (I John 3:16). "How great is the love the Father has lavished on us, that we should be called children of God!" (I John 3:1).

With all the proclamations of God's love for us, why can't we believe? At one time I thought I could learn to love myself by memorizing all the pertinent Scriptures. It didn't work because I never dealt with the deeper issues in my life and, practically speaking, I wasn't living in obedience to the Word of God.

Let's say I have just returned from a Bible study on self-worth. I am filled with God's loving thoughts toward me. As I turn the key in the door, I am humming a song about being special to God. But as I step into the front hall, the song dies in my throat. Looking around I see the chaos my house is in because of my mad rush to get to Bible study by 9:00 a.m. Immediately I am filled with guilt and condemnation. Keeping a clean house has always been a battle and now my mind is filled with thoughts such as: *You're a lazy slob!* All those precious promises vanish faced with the reality of who I am as spoken to me through my home.

Or perhaps I stop at the store on the way home from Bible study. Just as I am reaching for a head of lettuce, I see Emily coming in the store. *Oh no,* I think as I duck behind the display of oranges, *I hope she doesn't see me.* Instantly old hurts and anger rise in my chest and I hurry to get out of the store before I meet her. In the car on the way home, I am ashamed of my knee-jerk type of reaction. I know that as a Christian I should be forgiving—after all, how can God forgive me if I won't forgive. The day is ruined. I forget that God loves me and I can only think of my failure. Why am I unable to forgive at the deep level required by Jesus?

Or perhaps I arrive at my friend's house at 8:55 a.m. for our 9:00 study. I am congratulating myself on being punctual as I hang my coat in the front hall closet, and am happily anticipating a morning of fellowship with friends. As I slide the closet door shut, I catch a glimpse of myself in the mirrored door. I see a woman who is about thirty pounds overweight with hair that is in need of a shampoo and set. My anticipation vanishes as I try to slip unnoticed into a back-row chair. My mind isn't on the lesson. Instead, I am furtively glancing at the other women, comparing myself and feeling very inferior. Rather than responding to the love in the Word of God, all I hear are words of condemnation. I leave with the distinct impression that I don't measure up.

When we feel pulled down by a poor self-image, we need to know the love of God. We need to believe that God sees us as very special. The emphasis is on believing rather than doing because we can't earn God's love. Also, the way we feel about ourselves determines our actions. If we see ourselves as successful, we will achieve success. But, if we aren't doing the things we know we should be doing, it is hard to like ourselves. As a result, we feel guilty and our self-esteem suffers. I might know in my head that my achievements don't make me righteous before God, but everything within me screams: "You are unworthy to receive God's love." And since it is only God's love that will set me free, a vicious cycle has been established. Somehow, I have to break that cycle, and the quickest way is to do whatever needs to be done, whether it is cleaning the house, asking forgiveness or losing the excess weight.

Now of course, this doesn't make us any more acceptable to God, but it does help us *feel* a little more acceptable. It stops our hearts from condemning us and we can begin to open up to the love and grace of God. We have broken that cycle and once God's love and grace start to shine in our hearts, we can begin to love ourselves.

For this reason, I have approached the whole idea of a good self-image from the aspect of doing. As to which comes first, the believing or the doing, we run into the same problem as the chicken and the egg. Right actions feed a right self-image which in turn engenders more right actions.

Just recently I was under the distinct impression that God wanted me to get up an hour earlier in the morning. I have never been a morning person and have a hard time talking before 9:00 a.m. A month went by and still I wasn't being obedient to that inner voice. As a result, I was conscious of my disobedience as soon as I got up in the morning. That subtle feeling of guilt persisted throughout the day. Other areas of my life were affected and it seemed I could never quite finish my household chores or spend the time I wanted in writing.

Finally, one night while lying in bed, I decided to make an agreement with God. I would get up, and use that hour for Bible reading and prayer. Soon I found that by my obedience in that area of my life, other things fell into place. First of all, my attitude changed. I awoke with a good feeling knowing I was being obedient. Second, I found I became more disciplined with other things—I began making those phone calls I hate to take the time for and answering the mail that had been piling up on my desk. The more I was obedient and disciplined, the better I felt about myself and the more I accomplished. It all started with one little act of obedience.

Somewhere along the way we pass from the doing to the believing. Sooner or later we have to realize that God loves us for who we are and not what we do for Him. Hopefully, this process will occur gradually as our right actions open us up to receive more and more of God's love and grace. These right actions should act like the supports of a building—holding the building up temporarily until the real foundation can be laid. Otherwise, like the Pharisees, we may become self-righteous keepers of the Law, proud of our accomplishments. No matter how much we do for God, Scripture tells us, "all that we have accomplished you have done for us" (Isaiah 26:12b). This was the secret of Paul's success. Although he probably accomplished more for God than any other man, he knew his achievement lay not in his striving but in the grace of God: " . . . I worked harder than all of them—yet not I, but the grace of God that was with me" (I Corinthians 15:10b).

Several years ago I found myself in the position of greatly decreased activity. Three of my four children left for college about mid-August. The summer had been frantic as we entertained many out-of-town visitors and adapted to several different schedules of work and summer sport leagues. Suddenly I found myself rattling around the house with a greatly reduced work load. I felt as if I had been transferred from a pressure chamber to a vacuum. I seemed to be expanding into empty space without purpose or goals.

I began to search for something to fill my time: Bible studies would not begin till October; I had just finished a book and had no direction on future projects; I had no speaking engagements on the calendar and my phone, which usually rang incessantly with calls for counseling, was silent. As August moved into September and my youngest child, Kelly, went back to high school, I found myself growing more and more depressed. I would wake up in the morning wondering what I would do to fill my day. I soon came to see that my identity was rooted more in the roles I fulfilled than in my personhood. Since I no longer felt needed as a mother, writer, speaker or counselor, I felt worthless and unlovable. My self-image fell to zero.

All the while God was working through my negative thought patterns and self-pity to show me that my real identity could only be found in Him. Little by little I started to relax and enjoy the oasis of quiet. Somewhere deep within my spirit I began to know that God's love for me was not contingent on my efforts. I also realized that the most important aspect of my life as a Christian was my personal, daily relationship with God—something that often suffered in the busyness of life.

My life is full again. By God's grace I made that transition from full- to part-time mother with a minimum of trauma. However, the lessons I learned during that three-month sabbatical have remained with me and my self-image is no longer totally dependent on my doing all the right things.

I suppose all of us who struggle with a poor self-image feel it is a curse of the "little" people and secretly envy those super Christians who seem so secure in the love of God. Certainly they never have to contend with feeling of low self-esteem; or do they?

On March 18, 1983, one of the most beloved and influential Christian women of our time went to be with the Lord. Catherine Marshall's writings have comforted and encouraged Christians for years. I'm sure most of us could never imagine Catherine battling with feelings of low self-esteem and yet, notes of her final days and months from her spiritual journal reveal just such a struggle.

On July 9, 1982, Catherine was rushed to Bethesda Memorial Hospital in Boynton Beach, Florida. For 32 days she remained in the Intensive Care Unit with tubes and machines handling all her bodily functions.

She was released to go home on August 4 but her recovery was very slow. Her loss of identity in the hospital, loss of speech (due to a tracheotomy) and loss of mental ability and memory for a period took it's toll on her self-image. In her journal she recounted her feelings during her convalescence:

> Since last summer, I have felt especially helpless and worthless—a digit. This has made it hard for me to accept God's unqualified love for me (He refuses to consider anyone a digit), and to accept completely the love and good will of others.

> Now God is cracking the whip. He is saying—"Start loving and let others love you so that you are fully ready to enter into resurrection life!"

This feeling of worthlessness, of being a "digit" made it difficult for Catherine to accept others' love and even the love of her husband, Len:

> Why was I often slow in accepting Len's love? And also the public's (through fan letters)? This means I have not fully accepted God's love either. When we don't accept His love, we cannot receive that of others.

The knowledge that we are not living up to our potential in Christ causes all of us feelings of failure and low self-worth but have we considered that even the Billy Grahams and Catherine Marshalls feel this gap between what they are doing and what they could achieve? Perhaps they feel it even more strongly because of the words of Scripture which tell us: "From everyone who has been given much, much will be demanded; and from the one who has been entrusted with much, much more will be asked (Luke 12:48b). Certainly this was a thought which troubled Catherine during her final days on earth. At one point she confessed: "I feel like I'm accomplishing so little." Her entry into her journal on October 9 reinforces this feeling:

> . . . Struggling with this thought: Because I have had such privilege and so many blessings in my life as a Christian, if I do not measure up to what is expected of me, I will not only let Jesus down, but all those people "out there" might think less of Him. Yet how completely silly to think that Jesus' reputation is dependent upon what I do!

A good self-image is not a static thing; it is not something we attain once and then have firmly fixed in our nature. No, it is more like a tightrope walker delicately balanced on a wire and swaying slightly as his balancing bar swings a little too much to the right and then to the left; there is an ever-present danger of leaning too far to one side and falling. Although none of us would enjoy the fall, it is not necessarily a bad thing. We would learn more about balance—what not to do—and also, that when we fall, there is a net beneath us: those "everlasting arms" (Deuteronomy 33:27) ready to catch us and put us back on the high wire again.

So many things can change our self-image: death, disability, acquiring new skills, having a baby, grown children leaving home; all require reassessment and re-evaluation. Change is part of all human experience, an opportunity to grow and learn flexibility and, above all, the grace of God that is available to us in each experience. The last entry in Catherine's journal, just a day before her death, records:

> This morning I was told most emphatically: "Keep your eyes off yourself, off your symptoms, off negatives, and look steadily at Me."

What a prescription for a good self-image: "Let us fix our eyes on Jesus, the author and perfecter of our faith" (Hebrews 12:2). None of us has "arrived," we are all in the process of becoming. When Enoch "arrived" he was promptly transported to the heavenly realm (Genesis 5:21-24). There are no perfect people on this earth; only imperfect vessels indwelt by a perfect Lord who is slowly but surely bringing us to perfection. There are no magic formulas, quick fixes or easy roads, but only by our "steadfastness and patient endurance we shall win the true life of our souls" (Luke 21:19, Amplified).

Ultimately, it is Jesus who will make us into the person we desire to be; the person that was chosen from all Eternity to "be for the praise of his glory" (Ephesians 1:12). As we see *His* image replacing *our* imperfect image we will truly begin to love the person we are becoming. Thank God for our imperfections and weaknesses; every weakness we have is an opportunity to demonstrate the power of God (II Corinthians 12:9), if only we keep our eyes on Him and not on ourselves. Our weaknesses, like Catherine's and Paul's, are but a reminder that it is only God's grace which will bring us to perfection so that none of us will be able to boast in His presence (Ephesians 2:9). Then we too, like Paul, will be able to say "I am what I am by the *grace* of God" (I Corinthians 15:10).